Carnegie Commission on Higher Education
Sponsored Research Reports

MODELS AND MAVERICKS:
A PROFILE OF PRIVATE LIBERAL ARTS
COLLEGES
Morris T. Keeton

BETWEEN TWO WORLDS:
A PROFILE OF NEGRO HIGHER EDUCATION
Frank Bowles and Frank A. DeCosta

BREAKING THE ACCESS BARRIERS:
A PROFILE OF TWO-YEAR COLLEGES
Leland L. Medsker and Dale Tillery

ANY PERSON, ANY STUDY:
AN ESSAY ON HIGHER EDUCATION IN THE
UNITED STATES
Eric Ashby

THE NEW DEPRESSION IN HIGHER
EDUCATION:
A STUDY OF FINANCIAL CONDITIONS AT 41
COLLEGES AND UNIVERSITIES
Earl F. Cheit

FINANCING MEDICAL EDUCATION:
AN ANALYSIS OF ALTERNATIVE POLICIES
AND MECHANISMS
Rashi Fein and Gerald I. Weber

HIGHER EDUCATION IN NINE COUNTRIES:
A COMPARATIVE STUDY OF COLLEGES AND
UNIVERSITIES ABROAD
*Barbara B. Burn, Philip G. Altbach, Clark Kerr,
and James A. Perkins*

BRIDGES TO UNDERSTANDING:
INTERNATIONAL PROGRAMS OF AMERICAN
COLLEGES AND UNIVERSITIES
Irwin T. Sanders and Jennifer C. Ward

GRADUATE AND PROFESSIONAL EDUCATION,
1980:
A SURVEY OF INSTITUTIONAL PLANS
Lewis B. Mayhew

THE AMERICAN COLLEGE AND AMERICAN
CULTURE:
SOCIALIZATION AS A FUNCTION OF HIGHER
EDUCATION
Oscar and Mary F. Handlin

RECENT ALUMNI AND HIGHER EDUCATION:
A SURVEY OF COLLEGE GRADUATES
Joe L. Spaeth and Andrew M. Greeley

CHANGE IN EDUCATIONAL POLICY:
SELF-STUDIES IN SELECTED COLLEGES AND
UNIVERSITIES
Dwight R. Ladd

STATE OFFICIALS AND HIGHER EDUCATION:
A SURVEY OF THE OPINIONS AND
EXPECTATIONS OF POLICY MAKERS IN NINE
STATES
Heinz Eulau and Harold Quinley

ACADEMIC DEGREE STRUCTURES:
INNOVATIVE APPROACHES
PRINCIPLES OF REFORM IN DEGREE
STRUCTURES IN THE UNITED STATES
Stephen H. Spurr

COLLEGES OF THE FORGOTTEN AMERICANS:
A PROFILE OF STATE COLLEGES AND
REGIONAL UNIVERSITIES
E. Alden Dunham

FROM BACKWATER TO MAINSTREAM:
A PROFILE OF CATHOLIC HIGHER
EDUCATION
Andrew M. Greeley

THE ECONOMICS OF THE MAJOR PRIVATE
UNIVERSITIES
William G. Bowen
(Out of print, but available from University Microfilms.)

THE FINANCE OF HIGHER EDUCATION
Howard R. Bowen
(Out of print, but available from University Microfilms.)

ALTERNATIVE METHODS OF FEDERAL
FUNDING FOR HIGHER EDUCATION
Ron Wolk

INVENTORY OF CURRENT RESEARCH ON
HIGHER EDUCATION 1968
Dale M. Heckman and Warren Bryan Martin

The following reprints and technical reports are available from the Carnegie Commission on Higher Education, 1947 Center Street, Berkeley, California 94704.

. . . AND WHAT PROFESSORS THINK: ABOUT STUDENT PROTEST AND MANNERS, MORALS, POLITICS, AND CHAOS ON THE CAMPUS, *by Seymour Martin Lipset and Everett Carll Ladd, Jr., reprinted from* PSYCHOLOGY TODAY, *November 1970.*

DEMAND AND SUPPLY IN U.S. HIGHER EDUCATION: A PROGRESS REPORT, *by Roy Radner and Leonard S. Miller, reprinted from* AMERICAN ECONOMIC REVIEW, *May 1970.*

THE UNHOLY ALLIANCE AGAINST THE CAMPUS, *by Kenneth Keniston and Michael Lerner, reprinted from* NEW YORK TIMES MAGAZINE, *November 8, 1970, pp. 28–86.*

PRECARIOUS PROFESSORS: NEW PATTERNS OF REPRESENTATION, *by Joseph W. Garbarino, reprinted from* INDUSTRIAL RELATIONS, *vol. 10, no. 1, February 1971.*

RESOURCES FOR HIGHER EDUCATION: AN ECONOMIST'S VIEW, *by Theodore W. Schultz, reprinted from* JOURNAL OF POLITICAL ECONOMY, *vol. 76, no. 3, University of Chicago, May/ June 1968. (Out of print.)*

INDUSTRIAL RELATIONS AND UNIVERSITY RELATIONS, *by Clark Kerr, reprinted from* PROCEEDINGS OF THE 21ST ANNUAL WINTER MEETING OF THE INDUSTRIAL RELATIONS RESEARCH ASSOCIATION, *pp. 15–25. (Out of print.)*

NEW CHALLENGES TO THE COLLEGE AND UNIVERSITY, *by Clark Kerr, reprinted from Kermit Gordon (ed.),* AGENDA FOR THE NATION, *The Brookings Institution, Washington, D.C., 1968. (Out of print.)*

PRESIDENTIAL DISCONTENT, *by Clark Kerr, reprinted from David C. Nichols (ed.),* PERSPECTIVES ON CAMPUS TENSIONS: PAPERS PREPARED FOR THE SPECIAL COMMITTEE ON CAMPUS TENSIONS, *American Council on Education, Washington, D.C., September 1970. (Out of print.)*

STUDENT PROTEST—AN INSTITUTIONAL AND NATIONAL PROFILE, *by Harold Hodgkinson, reprinted from* THE RECORD, *vol. 71, no. 4, May 1970. (Out of print.)*

WHAT'S BUGGING THE STUDENTS?, *by Kenneth Keniston, reprinted from* EDUCATIONAL RECORD, *American Council on Education, Washington, D.C., Spring 1970. (Out of print.)*

THE POLITICS OF ACADEMIA, *by Seymour Martin Lipset, reprinted from David C. Nichols (ed.),* PERSPECTIVES ON CAMPUS TENSIONS: PAPERS PREPARED FOR THE SPECIAL COMMITTEE ON CAMPUS TENSIONS, *American Council on Education, Washington, D.C., September 1970. (Out of print.)*

Models and Mavericks

Models and Mavericks

A PROFILE OF PRIVATE LIBERAL ARTS COLLEGES

by Morris T. Keeton

Academic Vice-President, Antioch College

with a commentary by Katharine E. McBride

Sixth of a Series of Profiles Sponsored by

The Carnegie Commission on Higher Education

MCGRAW-HILL BOOK COMPANY

New York   St. Louis   San Francisco   Düsseldorf
London   Sydney   Toronto   Mexico   Panama
Johannesburg   Kuala Lumpur   Montreal
New Delhi   Rio de Janeiro   Singapore

The Carnegie Commission on Higher Education,
1947 Center Street, Berkeley, California 94704,
has sponsored preparation of this profile as a
part of a continuing effort to obtain and present
significant information for public discussion.
The views expressed are those of the author.

LA
227.3
.K4

MODELS AND MAVERICKS

A Profile of Private Liberal Arts Colleges

Copyright © 1971 by The Carnegie Foundation for
the Advancement of Teaching. All rights reserved.
Printed in the United States of America.

Library of Congress catalog card number 79-154242

123456789MAMM7987654321

07-010029-2

Foreword

The private liberal arts colleges dominated higher education in the United States for over two centuries. For the past century, however, they have experienced a comparative decline and now encompass about one in five of all students. This past century has belonged increasingly to the universities, the four-year colleges (usually state) that concentrate on training for specific occupations, and the community colleges. Yet the liberal arts colleges continue to hold a place of considerable influence and even leadership. They provide some of the highest-quality undergraduate institutions. They are the principal source of diversity and innovation. They set standards for concern with the welfare of the individual student. They serve as models for institutional autonomy. American higher education is enriched by their existence and their example. Private liberal arts colleges also face a renaissance, for they are by nature more adaptable to the new concerns of so many students, while the more massive institutions are clearly in greater trouble — some of them are turning to their own internal liberal arts colleges to respond to students' concerns.

Morris Keeton is well qualified to discuss this almost uniquely American type of institution of higher education. He has served liberal arts colleges in a very creative role and surveyed many others in depth. His thoughtful study looks at the problems of today and their solutions in the future.

Clark Kerr
Chairman
The Carnegie Commission
on Higher Education

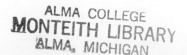
ALMA COLLEGE
MONTEITH LIBRARY
ALMA, MICHIGAN

Preface

This book focuses upon private independent colleges and Protestant-controlled colleges and offers recommendations on how these institutions might better serve our society. Colleges, in this context, are four-year undergraduate institutions whose dominant function is to offer baccalaureate studies. Some offer master's and doctoral work, but only as a secondary task.

Morris T. Keeton

Contents

Models and Mavericks

1. A Task for Private Colleges

In its first report the Carnegie Commission on Higher Education stated (1968, p. 1): "What the American nation needs and expects from higher education in the critical years just ahead can be summed up in two phrases: quality of result and equality of access." In a subsequent report on the finance of higher education, Howard R. Bowen (1968, pp. 2–3) spelled out a set of objectives which he believes to be fairly settled national policy: (1) rich opportunities for personal and vocational development of individuals, with priority for the advancement and dissemination of learning, (2) a system of maximally autonomous public and private institutions providing a diversity of programs for different types of students and different regions, with sources of support of the colleges sufficiently different that no interest group can dominate the whole, (3) access for all to higher education within their capacity, regardless of barriers of finance, race, national origin, religion, place of residence, or background, and (4) free choice of programs and institutions for students, within the limits of their qualifications.

The achievement of these objectives will require a substantial increase in the volume and the variety of opportunities for higher education, with constant culling and refinement of programs to assure efficiency and to reflect responsiveness to changing social purposes and new circumstances. This new volume and variety implies a need for increasing financial resources and for greater efficiency in their use. To justify the claim on these resources, institutions of higher education will have to achieve a more sophisticated division of labor than they have today and develop both more substantive cooperation and a degree of competition which gives students a greater choice of services than they have. Implied in turn are changes in the planning, financing, governance, and management of colleges—which will be enormously difficult. It is

1

by no means settled that the changes implicit in this transformation will gain either a timely public acceptance or welcome by the institutions which should effect them. Hardly a voice is raised against the objectives. Yet enormous obstacles confront legislators and college leaders who seek to implement them. In the ensuing chapters I will try to show why the objectives require the commitments indicated, what is involved in fulfilling them, and how the task of doing so can be approached with some hope of success.

The Role of Private Colleges The burden of making the transformation needed in American higher education cannot and should not all be borne by public institutions. Private colleges as a group should undertake a part of each of the two main services suggested by the Carnegie Commission's phrase "quality and equality." The first of these is to accept a share of the sheer increase in numbers of students who will seek higher education within the next decade, and do so on terms that are clearly advantageous to taxpayers and to state governments. The second is to undertake ventures in qualitative achievement for which the private colleges are peculiarly qualified. Each of these qualitative ventures should derive from one or another of the advantages inherent in the nature of the particular private college; for example, (1) its freedom to orient its life and curriculum to a philosophical or religious perspective which would be inappropriate or illegal for a state-supported college, (2) the opportunity for curricular and instructional achievements which derives from distinctive student characteristics, capital resources, or other assets of particular private colleges, and (3) the freedom open to certain private colleges to undertake socially needed but risky or unpopular innovations, a freedom deriving from the distinctive control of these colleges.

The Volume of Need It has been common until this decade for educators to assume that public universities and colleges should serve all students requiring higher education who could not conveniently be accommodated by private institutions. The private institutions might, in other words, increase their numbers for their own reasons or as a gesture of largess, but they were under no obligation to do so. Some even maintained that they were obligated not to grow because expansion caused risks to the quality and the security of their future. In spite of these assumptions, the increase in enrollment accepted in private colleges has been substantial (about 78.3 percent nationwide) between 1939–40 and 1967–68 (*Digest of*

Educational Statistics, 1969). (Data include both resident and extension-degree-credit students. "Private institutions" in this statistic include all private colleges and universities, sectarian and nonsectarian.)

The growth in enrollments and the rate of rise of costs per student have produced so substantial a burden upon taxpayers that the assumption of private college immunity from obligation to grow should be amended. I do not mean that every private college should add substantially to its numbers, but that as a sector of higher education the private college group should be expected collectively to plan with public institutions for a sharing of this responsibility.

Enrollment in higher education in 1967–68 was almost 6 million (full-time equivalent as distinguished from total head count given in Table 1). Half of the increase from the 50,000 of a century ago occurred between 1958 and 1967. Present trends are expected to produce a further increase of 2 million students within a decade; and the increase might reach 3 million if the Carnegie Commission's recommendations (1968, p. 3) on equalization of opportunity are put into effect. This would be a 50 percent further increase in total enrollment.

The rate of the rise of costs has been surprisingly steady for the past 20 years—5 percent per year compounded for all colleges and universities in this country, and 7.5 percent per year compounded for a group such as Chicago, Princeton, and Vanderbilt. Multiplying the increase of students by the increase of cost per student yields an annual growth of total educational and general expenditures of 12 percent per year for all universities from 1952 to 1964 (*Digest of Educational Statistics,* various years; and W. G. Bowen, 1968, pp. 3–21).

The proportion of the growth in costs borne by tax-supported institutions has steadily increased. Whereas 59 percent of students in 1957 were in public colleges and universities, the figure had risen to 69 percent by 1967. With a growing population and a

TABLE 1 *Enrollment in private institutions*

Year	Total (public and private)	Number in private institutions	Percentage of total in private institutions
1949–50	2,281,000	1,142,000	50.0
1967–68	6,928,000	2,036,000	29.4

NOTE: Includes universities.

SOURCE: *Digest of Educational Statistics,* 1969.

rising income per family, it might be supposed that it would be easier for citizens to meet the current costs of higher education than in less affluent times. The proportion of gross national product going into education, however, has risen from .56 percent in 1930 and 1.12 percent in 1960 (McGrath, 1966) to 2.46 percent in 1968–69, with a declining proportion of the total (now .89 percent) going to private higher education (Joint Economic Committee, 1969). Public officials, from members of local school boards to national congressmen, have felt a growing resistance to the needed tax increases and allocations. While education is still regarded as an outstanding investment for both the individual and the society, the pressure has grown to use every resource efficiently and to develop a reasoned basis for distributing the costs. This seems reasonable, and any recommendation about the role of private colleges should recognize these concerns for efficiency and for equity between public and private institutions in bearing the cost burdens.

Studies have been made or are under way in at least 24 states to devise plans for the efficient use of all institutional resources in higher education. An early effort along these lines was made in the state of New York.

One of the most persuasive studies is *Pluralism and Partnership* (1968), prepared for the Coordinating Board of the Texas College and University System. Estimating that even though 75 percent of Texas high school students have the capacity for further formal education, only about 43.5 percent will attend college by 1985, the study's staff projected costs to the state under a range of assumptions about the role of private colleges:

A Active support of a private college role by the Legislature and Coordinating Board — up to 25 percent of senior college enrollment might be in private institutions.

B Planning and cooperation, but not active pressure toward private enrollment — 18 to 20 percent of total enrollments would be in private colleges (present rate is 20.2 percent undergraduate, 26 percent graduate and professional).

C Hostile or neutral attitude by Legislature and Coordinating Board toward private colleges — 7 to 9 percent of enrollment might be in private colleges.

If private enrollment drops from the 1967 rate of 20.2 to 18 percent, the net additional cost to the state, which presumably will absorb a bigger proportion of the increased enrollment, will rise from $11 million in 1970 to $36 million in 1985. If private enrollment drops to only 10 percent, the added cost to the state will rise from $34 million in 1970 to about $183 million in 1985. The Liaison Committee on Texas Private Colleges and Universities has recommended, on the basis of these findings, that Texas would achieve a tax advantage if it supported a program of assistance to private colleges. That assistance would involve less cost than would the assimilation of excess enrollments into existing or new public campuses. This alternative would take the form of direct financial assistance to private colleges, which would enable them to meet rising costs.

In 1968, California's private colleges and universities served about 23 percent of the state's enrollment in four-year colleges and graduate and professional schools. The state of California appropriated $534 million for higher education in 1967–68 and was spared about $200 million (including debt service) spent by the private institutions. With voters rejecting further bonded indebtedness for new construction in a 1968 election and the state government pressing for tuition charges at the public universities, California would be hard pressed to meet the cost of its anticipated minimum enrollment increase if more than 80 percent of it is to be absorbed into the public institutions.

In the decade 1957 to 1967, California experienced a decline in the percentage of higher education enrollment in private institutions—from 31 to 23 percent. Even so, the state's private institutions during that period absorbed a 71 percent increase in student population—from 51,000 in 1957–58 to just under 87,000 in 1967–68. During the final five years of that decade, enrollment growth was at the rate of 6.2 percent per year. For the subsequent five years the projected growth rate is 3.9 percent annually—ranging from 2 to 3 percent for large institutions to 5 to 8 percent for smaller ones—as compared to the 6 to 7 percent anticipated by public institutions. Projecting an increased cost per student of 7 percent per year, these private institutions face a growing gap between income and expense even if they absorb less than their present share of total enrollment. Despite growth during the 1957–1965 period, four institutions had average annual operating deficits of over $50 per full-time student, and this number jumped to eight in 1966, and fourteen in 1967. While these institutions, for the most part, are not in serious difficulty financially, they are approaching the limit of their ability to give growing numbers of students the quality and type of education they presently offer (Association of Independent California Colleges and Universities, 1968).

Similar data are available for a growing number of states. All yield a similar finding: To continue the present systems of financing private and public institutions will be disadvantageous to both taxpayer and private institutions.

The Governor of New York in June, 1967, signed a bill which adds to the scholarship, grant, and loan provisions already available to individual students for use at institutions of their choice. The bill grants to the institution $400 per earned bachelor's or master's degree and $2,400 per earned doctorate awarded in the prior academic year—a provision estimated to produce about 5 percent of current operating budget for the private institutions. This precedent is important in that it permits a form of aid minimizing the necessity of specific state control and allowing for expansion of support in a way advantageous to the taxpayer, as long as the amounts are below the cost of the state's enrolling the added students in public institutions (ibid., pp. 5–7).

Assuming that constitutional questions involved in new forms of public support for private education can be resolved, there are forms of added public support which meet the criteria proposed by the Carnegie Commission (for federal support) and serve the objectives enunciated by Howard Bowen (1968, pp. 2–3). Even such measures as this cannot be expected to enable private institutions to reverse their trend toward a lower proportion of the enrollment (recently down to 29 percent). However, the rate of reduction might be arrested to produce a proportion for the next decade between 23 and 25 percent nationwide and a proportion not lower than 17 to 20 percent in such states as Texas and California. Even so, within the next decade the private institutions would face a substantially enlarged enrollment, perhaps in some states as much as from 40 to 50 percent.

While it clearly would be to the financial advantage of states and taxpayers to encourage increased enrollment for private colleges, it is not clear how the private institutions can manage the task. One must ask whether, qualitatively, this prospect should be encouraged.

2. Quality Based on Distinctive Philosophy

Until well into the nineteenth century, American higher education was collegiate education, and the colleges in turn were predominantly private. In the earliest days of these colleges, public support was common, and the Dartmouth case (Rudolph, 1962, p. 189) established that the courts of that time did not view such support as incompatible with thoroughgoing autonomy of the private board of trustees. This issue of the incompatibility of tax-based financing of colleges with their sectarian character had not been joined as it recently has been, for the idea of the separability of advanced study from the prevailing assumptions of philosophical and religious thought had not developed in more than a few minds, and in practice there were no institutions representing a genuine option to sectarian instruction.

The early American colleges performed, in relation to the vision of their own times, a heroic task against great odds. If they were subjected, however, to assessment against the objectives cited by Howard Bowen (1968) for our own next decade, they would prove defective on a staggering list of criteria: (1) the percentage of young people gaining access to college, (2) the commitment of students to learning, (3) the suitability of the curriculum and instruction for the variety of callings for which educated alumni were to be required, (4) the variety of qualifications of faculty needed for these curricula, (5) the maturing effects and characteristics needed in the life and environment of the colleges themselves, (6) the promptness with which new knowledge would continue to find expression in the curriculum, (7) the relevance of studies to the publicly perceived and student-perceived needs of the times, and especially to the immediate future, (8) the variety of learners and styles of intellectuality fostered within the colleges, and (9) the role of the colleges in the nurture of a pluralism of cultural inputs available for the enrichment of American society.

7

It would be unfair to apply to an earlier time criteria appropriate only to our own. But this way of looking at history brings sharply home the enormous evolution of function which higher education has undergone since colonial days. It suggests also that, in considering the qualitative demands of the next decade upon higher education, we should pay close attention to the changing cultural context.

The early American colleges are often thought to have represented a golden age in higher education, a time when scholarship in its purest and best sense was the driving force of the life of the college and when administration, faculty, students, and trustees were as one in their vision of education. This dream of past glory sometimes includes the idea that in those times anyone who really needed and wanted a college education could, by dint of courage and commitment, get one. Nothing could be farther from the truth.

Even as late as 1870, only 1.7 percent of the young people aged eighteen to twenty-one were enrolled in colleges and universities, and *that* even though there was a dramatically smaller total population than today. In 1970 half of the same age group were in college (Educational Policies Commission, 1957, pp. 22, 31). The first women were not admitted to college until Oberlin enrolled four female freshmen in 1837 (Fletcher, 1943, vol. 1, pp. 290–315, 373–385). Typical of the earlier attitudes was that of Yale, which in 1783 examined Lucinda Foote, aged twelve, and found her "fully qualified, except in regard to sex, to be received as a pupil of the Freshman class of Yale University" and accordingly turned her away (Woody, 1929, vol. 2, p. 137).

Students of the eighteenth- and early nineteenth-century colleges were both younger and more typically from wealthy or privileged families than in the mid-twentieth century. Entering students were viewed as pupils and boys. Fourteen-year-olds were common among the freshmen. Thus, a Portland newspaper of the 1820s accused the Bowdoin College faculty of "driving fourteen-year-old boys almost insane with anxiety and fear" (Hatch, 1927, p. 73). The youthful climate of some colleges was accentuated by the presence of an "academy" into which applicants unsuccessful in passing the entrance examinations were placed while they worked their way up to "college level." Thus the opening class of Antioch College in 1853 included only 8 college students, but over 150 academy enrollees (as attested by the first catalog). As to the social class origins of students of those days, Princeton in 1827 simultaneously reduced tuition and faculty salaries to help dispel its reputation as a rich man's college. President Day of Yale worried aloud about the moral and religious tone of a student body drawn too largely from the privileged orders. Generally, the colleges were fighting a losing battle to gain larger proportions of low-income students (Rudolph, 1962, pp. 197–199).

By the 1830s the makeup of the student bodies of colleges, on one hand, and the nature of the curriculum, on the other, were sufficiently incongruent that radical change was imminent. Conflicting demands for greater intellectuality in college life and for greater democratization of admissions were being pressed. Tracing these historical forces through their effects in curriculum, George Schmidt (1957, pp. 238–239) writes:

The liberal curriculum has come a long way since it began as the seven liberal arts salvaged from the wreckage of the Roman Empire. An accidental assemblage to begin with, it was pretty thin fare until enriched by the three philosophies of Aristotle in the high Middle Ages. The fifteenth and sixteenth centuries brought Greek into the program, and it became a standby from then on. The seventeenth century added mathematics, the eighteenth the first formalized instruction in science. It was at this stage in its development that the liberal curriculum reached America; this was substantially the curriculum that was hailed by the Yale Report of 1828 as *the* liberal education, which was sound and good for all time. Yet even in that approved form it included no extensive study of the Great Books, for there was not much time left for those after grammar, syntax, and routine translation had been attended to. The Yale report failed in the long run to fix the content of the liberal arts, for subject after subject that the conservative had thought secondary or quite unnecessary found its way into the college catalogues. Modern languages, English literature, and history all gained admission over bitter opposition and, once in the fold, became in turn staunch defenders of the revised *status quo*. By the end of the nineteenth century laboratory science had firmly established itself and even gained priority status: and the social sciences, economics, government, sociology were gaining recognition as worthy bearers of the Great Tradition. Each of these subjects in turn was constantly changing in content and emphasis. And the process goes on: to this day newly organized areas of knowledge and novel combinations of subject matter are shouldering their way into the select circle and gaining the grudging approval of the custodians of the cultural heritage. A day may come when such relative newcomers as the behavioral sciences and American studies will be defended to the death as essential to the liberal tradition, against the impudent claims of the Philistines of that day. The numbers of those who view this curricular evolution with alarm are declining, but the Hutchins school, for example, remains in opposition, and Catholic leaders are critical of the trend. At a recent meeting of the Association of American Colleges the Reverend Theodore M. Hesburgh, President of Notre Dame University, sharply denounced the submergence of the classics, that core of all liberal education, and deplored the resulting disintegration of the cultural unity of the Western World.

The colleges of our first two centuries were, for all their idealism, a highly practical tool for recruitment into the few professions then recognized (ministry, law, and medicine, primarily). They assured their graduates of certain opportunities for social leadership and status in a society which, though breaking with European traditions, was still relatively aristocratic. These colleges were a conservative social force, transmitting and upholding for the most part a mix of European and classical culture that was only partially suited to its own time, and even less to the times to come. The early American college students were often not selected on the basis of aptitude and were also often much less motivated as learners than today's students.

In terms of producing literate men whose increased social standing would make them political and business leaders, reproducing academics, training ministers, and preserving an inherited social order, the early American colleges were highly successful. Admittedly, the colleges did not necessarily produce persons with free, inquiring minds, in our sense of those terms, but this was not their aim. Colleges produced for the most part Christian gentlemen who would fit into and further the status quo. College was open to students of considerably younger age. Colleges then were caretakers for the souls and minds of adolescents. As George Schmidt (ibid., pp. 86–87) describes the scene:

In their role as moral guardians of youth, college officers vacillated between an optimistic perfectionism and the more easily verifiable doctrine of total human depravity. . . . All seniors listened to lectures on evidences of Christianity. Standing *in loco parentis* and, by inference, *in loco dei,* presidents and faculties could make impressive use of morning and evening prayers to appeal to the better instincts of their captive audiences, or to threaten them with the wrath of God.

Generally speaking, the history of American colleges has been one of resistance to reforms of curricula and governance. External pressures were largely instrumental in forcing needed changes, though some historians credit students in the early nineteenth century with having had considerable effect on the liberalization of curriculum. In any case, the current era is one in which internal leadership for such reforms is more widespread than in any previous period of American history.

Historically the American undergraduate college has been a highly protective (in George Stern's sense), authoritarian society. It was relatively personalized only because it was small enough and still agricultural or pastoral enough to foster a climate of protectiveness. Perhaps the religious tone of most colleges also contributed to this effect. Even the faculty, however, had small standing or authority in matters of institutional governance— other than control over their own students' instruction and some matters of curriculum. Not until 1915 did the American Association of University Professors begin the fight for a contemporary form of academic freedom, and only after several more decades did faculty rights begin to be defined. The first nationally sponsored statement of student rights with strong establishment support and a substantial declaration for student voice in governance came in the last half of the 1960s.

The instruction of the early American colleges was largely oriented toward the past. With the reforms of the 1830s and the land-grant university movement, this pattern began a new period of change. The rapid development of science instruction since the 1920s and more recently the rise of the social sciences and the arts have sharply changed the content of liberal education.

The notion of intellectuality has undergone a fantastic transformation during the short history of American higher education. In the colonial college, students were drilled in the correct answers. With the nineteenth-century reforms new disciplines and sometimes new answers to older questions surfaced. At some point in this history, college began to be a place to question accepted truths on crucial issues (though not all colleges even today encourage this questioning). Further, since the mid-fifties the styles of intellectualism have come to include those of artists, who were previously thought to be creatures of feeling.

The earliest colonial colleges all represented substantially the same culture. In one colony the college was Presbyterian, in another Catholic or Unitarian, but the culture was one. Beginning with the land-grant universities, this ceased to be as clearly the case. The predominantly or exclusively Negro colleges also constituted an exception. By the mid-twentieth century we began to get universities so large that they contained distinctive subcultures within themselves, and the life of learning came to be even more different things to different people.

At the same time, a large number of private colleges, with distinctive boards of control, have supplemented the "multiversity" with its subcultures, and this has produced the opportunity for great cultural diversity within higher education. It is my belief that if education is to enlarge the scope of human possibilities, it must not be a homogenized world, but one of great cultural pluralism and interaction among cultures. To make American society a leader in the search for a better life, American private colleges should be in the vanguard of the creators of institutions of quality representing diverse concepts of excellence—diverse both in philosophic outlook and in educational programs.

QUALITATIVE VENTURES FOR PRIVATE COLLEGES

How can private colleges turn from their historic habit of reluctant response to external pressures for reform toward a pattern of active and intelligent leadership in improvement? To do so, the colleges will have to understand both the emerging needs of the society and their own limitations and capabilities. Three features of private colleges, taken collectively, provide a basis for discussing ventures for improving the quality of higher education: (1) their freedom to orient life and curriculum around a philosophical or religious perspective inappropriate for a state institution, (2) distinctive student characteristics, capital resources, and other assets, and (3) their freedom, because of their particular interests and orientations, to undertake socially needed but risky or unpopular innovations.

Philosophical and Religious Perspectives

The context for philosophical diversity

It is often supposed that religious or philosophic commitment severely inhibits a liberal education and that only neutrality with respect to value issues is compatible with genuine and effective inquiry. The passionate, almost dogmatic, persistence of some of the most creative men, whose inquiry in most instances defied their own traditions, should give pause to advocates of such neutralism. So, too, would a close acquaintance with, for example, both Ohio State University and Humboldt University (in East Berlin) where the roster of public speakers leaves something to be desired in terms of stimulus to serious study of alien philosophies.

The remedy is not to erase all philosophic distinctiveness from every university, but to assure awareness of both the dominant and alternative outlooks, to provide options for students and faculty within the nation's system of colleges, and to use the resources for communication within our society to further the testing of these outlooks.

From the perspective of optimizing learning and offering a spectrum of intellectual outlooks to test, the United States is fortunate to have institutions of higher education that differ markedly. We should sustain and enrich this variety.

The earliest American colleges were founded under religious auspices. In seventeenth-century America it did not occur to community leaders to think of separating religious instruction from intellectual development. Generally it was a key purpose of the college to train ministers, and so a substantial part of the curriculum was devoted to theology. Doctrine then conditioned inquiry. The far-ranging skeptical inquiries in religion and philosophy in liberal Protestant colleges today would have been regarded as scandalous even in the mid-nineteenth century.

For Harvard, and for many of its counterparts founded on sharply defined religious traditions, doctrine now shapes only a small part of the curriculum. Still a number of fundamentalist or conservative Protestant and other church-related institutions serve a function comparable to that of Harvard in the 1600s. Though a disciple of Sartre or Dewey might brand that function useless, this much must be conceded: These institutions serve their students by providing environments philosophically and culturally congenial with their own convictions and habits and, at the same time, offer students a stimulus to inquiry and speculation. The provision of such opportunity is in keeping with the precepts of the American Constitution and with our tradition of pluralism. In any case, a critique of any college's curriculum should be directed, not toward that institution's philosophy, but rather toward the worth of its instruction as judged from within the philosophy.

On many American campuses today there have arisen Marxist or post-Marxist "radical studies" groups whose ideals and philosophical perspectives are alien to those prevailing in our system of higher education. Although such groups do not seek written pledges of allegiance from faculty and student members, they have effective ways of screening for congeniality of perspective. Many a college administration would like to exclude them from campus altogether if it could do so within the bounds of the American traditions of academic freedom. These administrations tolerate the radical groups only on the assumption that in the free marketplace of ideas such groups will eventually be defeated.

This attitude of hostility toward "radical studies" does not fit our ideal of an interdependent society in which hostile and disparate philosophical and religious perspectives and cultures are allowed to thrive and compete with one another.

Rather than systematically starve "radical study," our society might encourage the development of colleges that operate within this framework and thus gain a perspective on the defects and advantages of these institutions. Not only would the alternative encourage diversity, which can have but a limited value when taken merely for the interest of diversity itself, but this alternative would make the radical segment's challenge more direct than otherwise. "Radical study" thus would test the present system of higher education, not through brush-fire wars, which are so often debilitating for all parties, but through direct engagement with the system and society, a situation that would enable each party to measure the other more precisely.

Diverse philosophical orientations

Wheaton College in Illinois has a double aim: liberal education and evangelical Christianity. For the majority of students, it provides solid undergraduate education, increased awareness of the artistic and intellectual world, more sophisticated Biblical and philosophical undergirding for their religious beliefs, and more complex and informed social and political attitudes than they had at entrance. Being affiliated with no one church, Wheaton is nevertheless (as alumnus Billy Graham put it) "a citadel of evangelical faith and fervor."[1]

Wheaton, I emphasize, is not a denominational college. Yet in its demands of faculty and trustees it enforces a religious perspective which would not be compatible with state control; for example, faculty must annually sign a religious creed. It is eligible for federal support, though its own policies limit its acceptance to a few types of help such as National Science Foundation equipment grants and undergraduate science research support. Wheaton is able

[1] A vignette of the Wheaton College of 1965–66 was published in Keeton and Hilberry, 1969, pp. 17–50.

to be selective in admissions (average 1965 Scholastic Aptitude Test (SAT) scores of 558 Verbal, 608 Mathematical Aptitude for men; 591 Verbal and 585 Mathematical Aptitude for women). Its strong academic drive produces students who win a significant share of national distinctions. It has its pick of faculty candidates among those who share its evangelical convictions. It charges a modest tuition and is able, with the aid of a dozen or so field representatives, to muster both annual contributions that balance the operating budget and large gifts to enrich its endowment and its plant fund.

A number of conservative or fundamentalist Protestant institutions thrive without having Wheaton's selectivity of students or faculty or its quality of academic achievement. They share with Wheaton the interplay of the drive for spiritual growth, on the one hand, and induction into "the processes of searching investigation" and the concern for general education, on the other; but their function, in the spectrum of institutions of higher education, seems distinct. Azusa Pacific College in California and John Brown University in Siloam Springs, Arkansas, are illustrative of this group. The former, founded in 1899 and first chartered to give the bachelor's degree in 1939, merged in 1965 with neighboring Los Angeles Pacific College, which had similar goals and spirit. Though not owned or controlled by any one denomination, it is the "Official College of the Church of God in the Southwest." Its president describes it as a "specific miracle college" whose motto is "God First." Though not asked to sign a specific creed as at Wheaton, a faculty member is expected to "belong to the fellowship of Christian believers . . . be an active participant in the work of some church . . . [and] express Christian meaning in his whole life." In Azusa and in John Brown about half of the required general education courses have a specific Christian emphasis such as "dynamic of the gospel," "relevance of the gospel," and "development of the gospel." Liberal education is defined as including "specific instruction pertaining to the Christian faith." At the same time the college recognizes the aim of liberal education as enabling the students to enjoy "cultural and intellectual freedom."

John Brown University, reflecting the personality of its founder (John E. Brown, Sr.), stresses the production of graduates of tremendous Christian zeal, strong mind, and titanic drive toward "productive work." Its students are average in ability: 500 SAT-V and 500 SAT-M for 1966–67. To supplement its courses of instruction, the college offers Sunday worship services, weekday chapel hours, weekly prayer meetings, student Christian organizations, special evangelistic services, and missionary and Bible conferences. Distinctive within this group of colleges is John Brown's stress upon vocational experience: All students engage in "employment type work experiences which supplement the studies."

Religiously distinctive colleges which are nondenominational (hence private independent rather than church-controlled) are, of course, by no means all predominantly conservative or fundamentalist in outlook. Even some colleges with a denominational voice in the appointment of trustees or in some other key part of governance or management are in fact independent of all but nominal and occasional efforts to inject any sectarian influence into the life of the institution. Yet such colleges at their best exhibit a pervasive religious character. Earlham, also subjected to intensive study in 1965–66, illustrates this. Earlham's internationalism, its opposition to war, its trust in decision by consensus, and its stress on "community" derive from and express its Quaker heritage and commitment. A recent entering class (1965) scored averages of 573 on SAT-V and 606 on SAT-M for men; 593 V and 598 M for women. Coupled with its strong intellectual drive and its selectivity of students and faculty, these prevailing commitments contribute markedly to the inquiry and to the intellectual tone of the campus. Perhaps the Quaker stress on seeking "that of God in every man" encourages individualism in intellectual search.

The varieties of religious and philosophical perspective which might govern institutions of higher education are by no means confined to the extremes of the Wheaton-like or the post-Marxist type of outlook. Consider an institution such as Goddard College, which has been explicitly committed to a particular variety of Deweyan philosophy of education. Even in the judgment of a critic hostile to its outlook (as in Paul Dressel's review of the college in Keeton and Hilberry, 1969, pp. 223–230), the presence of such a college within the system of higher education is not only of benefit to its immediate clientele but also to the productivity of the system of higher education as a whole:

One searches the Goddard catalog in vain to find courses and departments. Learning at Goddard is expected to occur in relation to a question or problem of concern to the learner. . . . Traditional areas of study are suggested by the use of subject-matter terminology, but no program of required fields and sequences of courses is anywhere evident.

. . . At Goddard, knowledge has value only as it is related to understanding and solving problems. The student learns through engaging in a wide variety of experiences; thus formal distinctions between course work and other types of learning experiences become meaningless. The individual must come to accept the responsibility for understanding and dealing effectively with his own problems and those of society. The college not only must encourage such behavior in the student; it must itself exhibit such behavior.

. . . Rules and restraints are held to a minimum. Goddard has never had grades. In a sense, of course, this very absence of specific rules constitutes a severe set of restraints, as is evidenced by the difficulties that many students have in adjusting to such a situation. . . . One member of the faculty characterized Goddard as a natural-selection process weeding out those who are incapable of self-direction and self-discipline and retaining those who are truly independent. . . . Goddard has developed a pattern of education which is definitely apart from the mainstream of American higher education and which therefore requires for its success both a type of student (average SAT scores of 586 V and 534 M for 1965) and a type of teacher that are not easily found. . . .

Another example of socially needed but unpopular development in higher education is an effective response to the call for Afro-American studies or black studies. In one sense, public universities have been highly responsive to the demands for correction of the bias of traditional curricula in respect to the Afro-American heritage; but when we come to the question whether genuine control over curricular decisions, particularly policy options, will be accorded to people who represent distinctive cultures that have developed within Negro America, public institutions are highly restricted as to the freedom they will accord black students and faculty to develop organization, policies, and program which reflect these disparate social perspectives and values. In this instance one might say that the chances that something genuinely innovative, something distinctive, might develop under public auspices are better than usual. Widespread guilt in the country about the heritage of discrimination against Negroes has produced a readiness to rectify historical wrongs. The rectification, however, is too often seen to be compatible with maintaining essentially the value system which prevails now rather than with discovering or creating, out of Afro-American and other minority cultures, new subcultures which, though not segregated, are distinctive. Even the Roy Wilkinses and the James Farmers find it difficult to accept the possibility of such a culturally distinctive development and to accord it public blessing. Under these circumstances it seems likely that the most vigorous and fruitful exploration of such an alternative will have to occur under private auspices if it can occur at all.

The potential variety of perspectives which might govern colleges is legion. These are often impossible to label. Sometimes the personal style of an individual leader is dominant in the culture of a college and takes a form which surely would not be supportable in a public institution. The point is not to prescribe which form should be realized but to make graphic the possibilities which should be explored by the private colleges of our time.

Rationale for philosophic diversity

In presenting examples to illustrate the need for diversity in philosophic outlook among American colleges, I have already alluded to reasons for having such diversity. Among these are the rights of those who do not share conventional philosophic outlooks to exercise the option of distinctive organization. From the point of view of pedagogy, there is the crucial possibility that for many students learning proceeds more deeply, cogently, and rapidly under circumstances of congenial ideological sponsorship and climate.

From the perspective of the advancement of knowledge and scholarship, there is a further reason for favoring a system of higher education within which diverse philosophies have forum and favor. This is closely akin to the reasons advanced by John Stuart Mill for society's being a free and hospitable forum: Truth is more likely to emerge within such a marketplace of ideas than in more closely regulated and "sensibly controlled" settings.

One of the primary obstacles to the rapid development of knowledge is the tendency of highly competent people to become set in belief. Their competency springs in great part from wide knowledge and inventiveness *within a framework* of thought and working assumptions—to see matters from a different perspective, even hypothetically, is difficult for them.

A prime objection to diversity illustrates the difficulty just mentioned. When Marxist students or black studies protagonists arise to challenge conventional campuses, many faculty members react with the view that these students are uneducable. It is often admitted that these same students are analytically keen and have heads crammed with information, much of which is considered by their critics to be irrelevant to the issues that ought to be discussed. These students appear to be doctrinaire, irrational, incorrigible. The integrity of such students is often questioned because they are willing to junk the concepts of honesty and virtue held by our culture and charge us with being "prostitutes," "pimps," and "hypocrites" without integrity or consistency of value commitments. This kind of conflict is stimulating to the life of a university if it causes interaction that is mutually instructive. It is, however, debilitating to all parties and perspectives to be in a constant fight for their lives.

Applying these abstract considerations to cases in point, I doubt that our society will achieve new insights from the current radical and black critique until these perspectives can be embodied in educational institutions expressive of their outlook. While some public universities have been hospitable to black studies, the hospitality has generally been most carefully guarded to prevent "takeover." If what I am saying is sound, "takeover," in the sense of autonomy in the conduct of a full-scale undergraduate and graduate program of studies and research, is precisely what is needed. It is needed to further learning and to advance our knowledge of the defects and abiding values within the prevailing ethos.

It will be argued that the faculty and students pressing for curriculum under radical philosophies of the right or the left are doctrinaire and anti-intellectual and that, as such, they have no place in a genuine university or college. This, however, merely reenforces the point that while an accepted creed (including conventional ones) often pulls against the demands of free inquiry, it can be made to serve them if it occurs in the context of active interplay with opposing outlooks. To develop an intellectual outlook, it is necessary to work at least tentatively within a system that is subject to challenge. In every sound college education, however, the *Weltanschauung* itself should also be at times the object of scrutiny and doubt.

It may be argued that colleges with distinctive ideologies would serve liberal education more productively if they were subcommunities within a university rather than wholly autonomous, separate entities. This is sound. It does not follow, however, that a committed group should refrain from functioning if it cannot find a hospitable university or college.

A Mennonite group has been exploring for some years the idea of establishing "Mennonite houses" adjacent to the campuses of major public or private universities. The students in these houses would enroll as regular students in the adjacent universities and take most of their academic studies there. For a portion of their degree programs, however, they would study in the Mennonite house, and the life of their community in the house would be distinctively Mennonite. Such a venture is now in progress at Temple University in Philadelphia, which serves as the field center of a Mennonite college in Indiana. Some Catholic groups are reported to have similar houses adjacent to campuses. The home college of the sectarian house may award the degree, or a student might transfer at least some of his sectarian credit into the larger university wherever regulations permit. In either case the same purpose is accomplished: By way of the large university, the student is exposed to both outlook and detailed instruction in the mode of the prevailing culture or of another outlook or outlooks divergent from that of his "home"; and at the same time he is able to view subjects from the perspective of the house.

Thus, without elaborate arrangements or special legislation, the private group is able to provide access to a good undergraduate program, drawing upon a rich array of faculty and university resources, at a minimal expense and without undertaking major long-range financial commitments. If state and federal governments do not provide some relief to private endeavors, it is probable that more and more groups will draw upon this model.

For the prosperous sectarian campus which needs the stimulus of a more diverse and sometimes hostile critique of its own perspective, the field center at a secular university offers an attractive option. Requiring, or at least encouraging, each student to spend a semester or a year at such a distant center could substantially increase the stimulus to learning. It could lower the total costs of the individual student's education. It would surely stimulate reform within the home base's ideology. Insofar as Bob Jones University thinks it has a message for the rectification of the secular university, this vehicle would also provide Bob Jones a means of testing its mettle and training its missionaries.

A further variation upon this theme of access for the student to instruction within divergent ideological frames of reference is provided within a Southwest Ohio Project for the Study of Religion in Higher Education. In this case a consortium of 11 colleges and universities allows cross-registration to students of each member college with as many others of the group as that home college approves. The cross-registration, originally for courses in the study of religion, now extends widely through the curriculum of some nine of the member institutions who are also in the Dayton–Miami Valley Consortium of Colleges and Universities. The larger list includes a private independent college (Antioch College), three private Protestant colleges (Wilmington College, Wittenberg University, and Wilberforce University), a Catholic, a Protestant, and a Jewish seminary (St. Francis Seminary, United Theological Seminary, and Hebrew Union College), three state universities (Central State University, Wright State University, and Miami University of Ohio), and a Catholic university (University of Dayton). The faculties and instruction of all of these institutions are of long-standing recognition and accreditation. Among some of the geographically closer ones, a bus service facilitates student movement, some of which extends to the noncurricular life of their respective college communities.

The mechanisms by which exposure of students to conflicting cultural and philosophical outlooks shall occur are incidental to the objective we should keep in view. In today's world, a person is not fully educated unless he is able to think and see within more than one philosophic outlook. Commitment to a single vision may well be possible if it is comprehensive and detailed in its elaboration. But the capacity to get within the viewpoints of others is essential in a world of many cultures whose participants and leaders see and believe passionately in the ways they see and believe. There is a danger that the whole world will be made up of warring parochial and provincial factions, it is true. But the route for avoiding that fate is to provide mutual insight into disparate outlooks.

The rationale for culturally distinctive colleges has been put in this way by Kenneth Boulding (Keeton and Hilberry, 1969, pp. 411–412):

A major problem of the next century will be the preservation of subcultures within the "superculture" of a complex, highly organized world. This technological superculture will standardize goods, ensure efficiency, and spread a certain kind of rationality throughout the world. But it is bound to be incomplete. It cannot fulfill man's need for a full range of thought and feeling. It cannot generate the particularities of language, art, ritual, and social bond that give a culture its emotional drawing power and its aesthetic satisfaction. If people are to be deeply satisfied in a place, a community, or a way of life, it will be because of the union of this efficient superculture with an enhancing subculture. Furthermore, the superculture may well stagnate, become bureaucratic and ponderous, unless new energy and new perspectives are constantly introduced through conflict and hybridization among subcultures.

Up to this point, colleges have largely been servants of the superculture, introducing students to information, techniques, and language that will enable them to move outside their own town or trade or social group. With a solid knowledge of chemistry, a young man can find work almost anywhere in the country, perhaps anywhere in the world. With an easy command of standard English—one of the by-products of higher education—he can talk to the superculture in its own terms . . . we do not expect to see colleges desert this role. Indeed, we are arguing that college education should reach far more people than it does now, acquainting them with broadly accepted habits of thought and helping them to intellectual competence that will command respect anywhere in literate society. . . . But the time is ripe, we hold, for America's colleges consciously to combine this function with another. They must not only free students from the confines of their past but also teach them to relish that past, to respect the local, the particular—this place, this manner of talk, this belief, this odd but traditional way of acting. In short, it is the business of the colleges to preserve and even create subcultures within the superculture. This is a large order. Little is known about the ways in which creative enclaves are born and sustained, and many liberal arts colleges still tend to mistrust their differences. Yet our examination of . . . colleges makes it clear that an institution can create an identity of its own, a mixture of history and conviction that will help students to define themselves and will provoke the collision of ideas on which society lives.

3. Quality Based on Distinctive Resources

A second type of qualitative venture which I recommend for private colleges derives from the distinctive student characteristics, capital resources, faculty, and other assets of particular colleges which have unique opportunity to be models of excellence. The term "excellence" is meaningless unless linked with a concept of the "kind" of which it is an exemplar. In this case I refer, not to the philosophically, religiously, or culturally distinctive kinds discussed in the preceding chapter, but to patterns of excellence which are also being striven for in public colleges and universities. In this context the mix of students and even the distinctive local or regional setting is a resource to be weighed in planning for effectiveness in achieving the college's purposes.

The question arises at once: Do private colleges have the unusual resources prerequisite to this function? Some do. Others do not. The evidence on this point is twofold: results already achieved, and data which appear to correlate with these results and to give some hints as to the dynamic underlying the results.

PRIVATE COLLEGE CAPABILITY FOR EXCELLENCE In a recent sketch of the current system of higher education in America, Clark Kerr (1968, p. 243) described the initial element as:

A strong segment — numbering half of all of the institutions of higher education, and including one-third of the students, about half of the universities of greatest prestige, and nearly all of the leading colleges — which sets standards for autonomy and quality and provides much of the innovative effort.

The part of this private segment under discussion here is a group of colleges that are predominantly undergraduate and either private independent or religiously controlled and non-Catholic.

Using 1968 data, the staff of the Carnegie Commission on Higher Education classified 700 institutions as liberal arts colleges—a listing which of course includes Catholic institutions (Appendix D). Of these, 118 were classified as "Liberal Arts Colleges, I"; that is, they either scored 60 or above on Astin's selectivity index (Science Research Associates, 1965) or were in the list of 300 leading baccalaureate-granting institutions in terms of the numbers of their graduates receiving Ph.D.'s at 40 leading doctorate-granting institutions from 1958 to 1966 (National Academy of Sciences, 1967). Combined, the private independent and Protestant colleges comprise 76 percent of the Carnegie Commission staff's list of selective colleges. Among these were about 1 out of 14 of the Catholic colleges, 1 out of 10 of the Protestant colleges, and over 1 out of 3 of the private independent colleges.

Private colleges do contribute to the quality of American higher education, but what is their contribution? How is it made?

The public colleges, with their mandate to open the door as widely as possible, reduce the likelihood that a high percentage of their graduates will go on to doctoral studies. For most students of these institutions, the highest quality of service they could receive would not be preparation for graduate school. Moreover, since the more selective colleges receive such qualified students at the outset, it is not clear what additional value the colleges contribute toward enabling their graduates to advance to the doctorate.

Two points thus emerge to guide the struggle for quality: Different criteria of quality are needed for colleges serving different types of students or different functions for their types of students.

TABLE 2 *Control and selectivity of private liberal arts colleges*

Type of control	Number of colleges	Percentage of total	Number of selective colleges	Percentage of selective colleges
Private independent	225	32.1	76	64.1
Private, Catholic	191	27.3	14	11.9
Private, with other religious affiliation	284	40.6	28	24.0
TOTALS	700	100.0	118	100.0

SOURCE: Carnegie Commission on Higher Education.

The most successful of whatever kind will be the colleges which induce in those admitted the learning and growth called for by such functions.

To deserve to survive, then, a private college need not be highly selective or focused upon predoctoral studies, but it should have a distinctive environment that is better than ordinary for evoking learning among the students it serves. It should know itself and its students. It should also know what service it intends to provide those students and what students can make best use of that service. Since a college cannot altogether control those entering its doors, the discovery of a function and a clientele which go together is often difficult.

Knowing the function and appropriate clientele is as much a matter of resolution as of recognition of facts. In the present state of knowledge, it cannot be said that we know enough to define such matches with confidence. Research on the impact of different colleges upon students raises more questions than it can now settle. Yet it is clearer than a decade or two ago what some of the limits are within which to seek the productive match. Thoughtful ventures in matching college and program to students, such as brand new campuses or thoughtfully designed amendments of plans for on-going colleges, should take into account such "givens" as the college's own opportunities and resources, on one hand and, on the other hand, the relevant research on the bearing of student input, college characteristics, and the interaction of the two upon learning.

What is there about the characteristics, resources, and limitations that makes them important? For the present discussion, I will focus upon the suggestion already cited that a productive campus offers a sufficient challenge to its clientele to open them to learning and change. The question for the individual college then becomes: How can it affect its students in this way? Given the heavy demand for higher education, this means that the vast majority of colleges have a potentially important function if they will but identify it and pursue it intelligently. They cannot, however, all become Oberlins, Sarah Lawrences, or Amhersts. The need for diversity is much greater than this; and the diversity ranges over modes and levels of intellectual style and ability as well as over socio-economic background factors, personality types, and vocational aspirations of students. A really outstanding "second chance" college for "late bloomers" or "turned off" students may be as important to the society and to the higher education system as the prestigious institution.

The Knapp-Goodrich Study Let me illustrate this need for diversity with an early study of productivity which was the work of R. H. Knapp and H. B. Goodrich (1952, pp. 260–261). The criterion of excellence under discussion was the rate per thousand at which male graduates in the period 1924 to 1934 continued to the doctoral level in science.

A consideration of the fifty highest-ranking institutions of the nation (1924–34) is particularly suggestive in revealing the types of institutions that have been especially productive of scientists. Of these fifty, forty are small liberal arts colleges, many of limited reputation, and mostly located in the Middle and Far West. Four are state-supported institutions devoted to engineering and especially to applied biological sciences. Only three are universities of eminent reputation, namely, Johns Hopkins, Chicago, and Wisconsin. The list is completed with the California Institute of Technology and three smaller universities of technological leanings, Brigham Young, Clark, and Rochester. The striking feature of this list is the comparative absence of technological schools and larger universities of high reputation. The liberal arts colleges, which constitute but a third of the institutions considered, account for 80 per cent of the first fifty.

In a search for explanation of these results, the Knapp-Goodrich staff identified three groups of colleges typified in quite distinct ways: (a) a foursome with broad intellectual emphasis (Reed, Oberlin, Swarthmore, and Antioch) showing the highest productivity; (b) a distinctive group of five men's liberal arts colleges (Amherst, Haverford, Wabash, Wesleyan University and Williams), less uniformly productive than the first group by the 1930s, but with a period of greatest effectiveness before the First World War; and (c) seven coeducational colleges of the Midwest and West which were among the most productive of the nation in that period (Central in Missouri, Colorado College, Cornell in Iowa, Earlham in Indiana, Kalamazoo in Michigan, Marietta in Ohio, and Whitman in Washington).

The criteria for the three groups were:

Group A: Broadly Intellectual

a Intense dedication to intellectual objectives

b Corresponding lack of preoccupation with social life and intercollegiate athletics c   A spirit of vanguardism or missionary zeal

d   A general quality of autonomy pervading administrative and disciplinary affairs

e   Unique curricular features designed to emphasize individual initiative and consideration of the individual

f   A propensity toward broad achievement in social science and humanistic studies as well as science

g   Evidence of marked selection of student body both for intellectual abilities and intellectual motivations

Group B: Affluent Men's

a   All-male student bodies

b   Conspicuously high costs of attendance

c   Greater wealth and usually superior physical facilities

d   Protracted history of achievement in the training of scientists

e   Comparative lack of distinction in this respect in recent decades

f   Well-paid faculties having the highest professional qualifications

g   Intellectually select student bodies of cosmopolitan and sophisticated type, frequently from wealthier homes

h   Strong traditionalist leanings

Group C: Western Protestant

a   Comparatively modest financial resources

b   Student bodies of only average general intellectual distinction

c   History of strong Protestant affiliation in most cases surviving in force

d   Tendency to attract students largely from immediately surrounding territories

e   Absence of marked faculty or student autonomy; frequently severe social and moral standards

f   Location in the Middle and Far West

g   Tendency to specific achievement in scientific training and propensity of students to elect science concentration more frequently

To me, this charting of observations suggests that these colleges, all effective in different ways, had combined some matters over which they had partial control with an acceptance of (or even commitment to) others over which they had little or no control, and a productive combination had evolved.

The facts about productivity in the Knapp-Goodrich definition of it have changed. Other measures of productivity and impact are more relevant today. The study nevertheless underscores the point that we are on the verge of knowing enough both to help colleges choose their own special modes of excellence and to help students choose colleges likely to offer the particular service they seek.

American Council on Education Survey

Since the Knapp-Goodrich study, much has been learned to complicate the task of creating an excellent college. In the current study we have considered two types of data on the students, faculty, administrators, resources, and other assets of private colleges. One of these types of data is drawn from aggregate studies, e.g., the American Council on Education 1967 survey of entering college freshmen and the National Opinion Research Center alumni survey. The other type of data is case material from individual colleges. The aggregate data tend to obscure distinctiveness of individual colleges or groups. Since our purpose here is to point out distinctive capabilities of individual institutions or groups of institutions, the case data help to get this possibility into clearer focus than would the aggregate data alone.

The entering students of a college are one of its major resources or inputs. A college environment with a higher than normal proportion of bright and creative students probably tends to stimulate greater than average growth and learning in average students. The ACE 1967 survey of entering freshmen enables us to say how private college students differ at entrance from the totality of entering students in the United States. We extract here from data on the competencies and experiences of 3,178 freshmen at large liberal arts colleges, 15,562 freshmen at small liberal arts colleges, and 11,709 freshmen at visibly Protestant colleges. We compare these three groups with national norms from a cross section of all 1967 college entrants in the United States.[1]

[1] These data were supplied to me by Dr. Howard Bobren, formerly of the staff of the Carnegie Commission on Higher Education, who in turn received them from the ACE with permission for us to use them. Work on statistical analysis to locate significant differences and to write up those differences with apparent importance for the question here discussed was done by Mrs. Nancy Teepen, research associate at Antioch College (Yellow Springs, Ohio), and by Miss Irene Saal, research assistant and Antioch student at the Antioch-Columbia Field Studies Center (Columbia, Maryland). Tables with technical explanation of our

In general, the three private college groups admitted students who had, by comparison with the United States cross section, higher high school grade averages, more scholastic and creative accomplishments on record, and more leadership experience within the school context. The private college freshmen had more highly educated parents than usual, often businessmen and professionals with higher than normal income, and these freshmen were more often financially dependent upon their families than usual. A much larger percentage were financing their freshman year partially through scholarships, grants, or other gifts, and a greater than average percentage felt no concern about financing their education. The girls among them were somewhat younger than the national norm.

Among the factors that are hypothesized to affect significantly the impact of a college upon its students are the aspirations and the previous experiences of its students. In this domain, as well as in that of ability and background reported in the previous paragraph, the private colleges have distinctive students. With the exception of technical skills such as programming a computer, typing, using a sewing machine, and developing and printing photographs, the private college freshmen had a wider range of competencies, particularly in sports and the arts, and a wider range of social experiences such as tutoring another student, discussing politics, and playing bridge. More private independent college freshmen had seen a foreign movie and participated in a demonstration within the previous year, and a greater than average percentage in all three private college groups had visited an art gallery or museum and taken a trip of 500 miles or more during that year. The private college freshmen had the edge on others in frequency with which there were personal relationships with their

---

processes of analysis and inference making are given in Appendix A. I have interpolated my own interpretive comments.

The ACE sample used above contains a larger proportion of selective colleges (defined on page 24) than is typical. In a complete list of 1968 colleges, 10 percent of the Protestant colleges are highly selective; whereas over 46 percent of the smaller ACE sample is drawn from a list of selective colleges. Among private independent colleges of 1968, about 34 percent are highly selective, but over 74 percent of the private independent colleges in the ACE sample are highly selective. The effect of the sampling is probably to represent the visibly Protestant colleges as more like the private independent colleges than a more representative sample would be.

teachers, whether the relationships consisted of arguing with them, being invited to their homes as guests, or asking their advice.

Some of the data suggest that there is an abnormally high tendency among private college freshmen to explore, to delay or suspend judgment, and to choose life work in which exploration and suspension of judgment are effective behavior. For example, independent liberal arts and Protestant college freshmen were more likely to be undecided about their prospective career choices, to have tried out "going steady" in high school, and to consider it very important to become expert in their fields. More than average numbers of them planned to go on to M.A.'s, Ph.D.'s, and M.D.'s, but considered it likely that they would change their major field and career choice during college. They chose business, education, and engineering less often than usual as their probable major field, and tended rather toward the humanities and the social sciences (especially history and political science) and toward preprofessional training.

Further evidence on the aspirations and attitudes of these freshmen emerges indirectly in certain survey items. The single factor most influential in the private college freshman's choice of college was its academic reputation. This difference was very substantial. The influence of parents, teachers, counselors, and friends attending the college upon this choice was about the same as the norm, but that of college representatives and alumni somewhat greater than normal—a hint of independence on the part of the student in hearing strangers and making up his own mind. A greater than average percentage of these entrants had applied to four or five other colleges and had been accepted at two or three of them. For them it was more important than usual to have the opportunity to live away from home and to participate in the social life of the college. By contrast, for the normal American freshman, low cost was the most important factor in college choice after the college's academic reputation and the influence of parents and teachers. Low cost and a counseling service least often influenced private college entrants crucially. In all three private college groups, a much greater percentage than average thought it likely that they would join social fraternities or sororities. A greater percentage of small liberal arts and Protestant college freshmen (as distinguished from large independent private college freshmen) were influenced by the thought that most students would be generally like them.

Freshmen at independent liberal arts colleges most frequently thought that their beliefs differed from those of other people (the contrast here applies to Protestant college as well as public college freshmen). But all three private college groups thought less often than average that the voting age should be 18; in this respect they were more conservative than average.

The private college freshmen differed among themselves between small and large independent college entrants, and between each of these and Protestant college entrants. Although all three groups had a wider than normal range of competencies, the specific areas of their competence were not always the same. Large independent college freshmen could more often describe the difference between stocks and bonds, mix dry martinis, do 15 push-ups, or name the players of a professional athletic team. Some of these data may have more to do with affluence than with intellectuality, or with privilege than with merit. They also raise the question of whether conventional excellence may, in some measure, be a reflection of class-bound standards which are irrelevant to the intellectual needs of society but which operate to impose handicaps upon those who have the capability for leadership but come from lower-class or racially and culturally distinctive groups.

Of the three private college groups, only small independent college freshmen were above average in reciting passages from memory or speaking a second language. Protestant college freshmen were above average in the use of *Robert's Rules of Order* and, along with large independent college entrants, in describing the Bill of Rights and using a slide rule. Both small and large independent college freshmen outshone Protestant college entrants in identifying architectural styles.

All three private college groups showed a high frequency of interest in keeping up with politics and developing a philosophy of life. More than average numbers of large independent college entrants thought it important to be an authority in their field; small independent college freshmen thought it important to be artistically and creatively accomplished; and Protestant college freshmen thought it important to become community leaders. More large independent college students thought it important to be well-off; small independent and Protestant college students more frequently placed importance upon helping other people and joining the Peace Corps or Vista. Being an expert in finance, not being obligated to other people, and succeeding in one's own business did not particularly appeal to freshmen at small independent and Protestant colleges but did appeal slightly better than the norm to students at large independent colleges. On specific issues, all three private college groups tended to hold more liberal opinions than did the norm, with Protestant college entrants as a group being more conservative than the other two. Independent college freshmen more often felt that colleges were not too lax on protests, that the college does not have the right to ban speakers, that student publications should not have to be cleared with college authorities, and that married women do not necessarily belong in the home. A simple "liberal-conservative" scheme, however, will not explain some of the data: The Protestant college students most often thought that large families should be discouraged. Large independent collegians seemed to be the most "hard-headed" of the three groups: They perceived the benefit of college as monetary (though not as often as the public college or total norms) and also thought for the most part that the individual cannot change society. (The large independent college entrants appear to be more typically of upper-income backgrounds, perhaps newly arrived, than are those of small independent or Protestant colleges.) In spite of the fact that the small independent and Protestant college entrants were more concerned than average with helping others, all three private college groups felt more strongly than average that disadvantaged people should *not* be given preferential treatment.

In summary, the ACE data fit a picture of private college students who are abler than average; have backgrounds more suited to a conventional type of success in college; and have aspirations, experiences, and attitudes geared to overcoming the hurdles typical of conventionally excellent colleges of liberal arts. (Tables of data are available in Appendix A of this profile.)

National Opinion Research Center Alumni Survey The NORC survey[2] enables us to compare the expectations of college which alumni recall having had and their present perceptions of how well or poorly these expectations were met. In this

[2] These results are from Survey #5023 of the NORC, University of Chicago, Chicago, Illinois. We are indebted to Father Andrew Greeley for permission to use the data. The initial statistical analysis and writeup in our own office were done by Mrs. Nancy R. Teepen. A further distillation was prepared by Miss Irene Saal. In choosing the particular data to report, we have used only statistically significant differences in reporting contrasts; but, since the large N produced a myriad of such differences, a still more stringent rule on size of difference has been imposed. See Appendix B for details.

study, independent colleges include both the small and the large private colleges treated in the ACE data just reported. The survey results were obtained from 8,035 alumni of the class of 1961, seven years after graduation. We are able to compare responses of alumni of private independent colleges with those of visibly Protestant colleges and with those of average alumni of all types of colleges. Allowance must be made for errors that may have crept into the returns because of respondents' inaccuracy of recall. The data are also perceptions of one category of participants in college, and they come from a period of college experiences that in some respects are quite different from the experiences of students of the late sixties. Nevertheless, for a view of the possibilities and problems of private colleges, these data are significant.

There are three highlights in the data:

1 Expectations of independent college graduates more frequently matched actual college experience than those of the Protestant college graduates or the average graduate of all types of colleges.

2 The congruency of aspirations and expectations of students and their perceptions of those of the faculty and officials of the college was greater in the private independent and Protestant colleges than in the general group. Student expectations were generally similar throughout all types of colleges, though naturally divergent in individual cases; but the private independent college is more often perceived to have delivered as expected than other institutions. The alumni of private independent and Protestant colleges had matched themselves to institutions in which they and the staff were pulling together. Allowing for the fact again that averages conceal dramatic variations among the individual institutions and subgroups of them and that we are dealing only with degrees and not with absolute differences, the private colleges reflect a greater fundamental congruity between aim and outcome. This holds true for both students and staff at these institutions.

3 Alumni of independent colleges gave their colleges high ratings on the quality of teaching and the competence of both faculty and fellow students.

Among the significant details within this picture, these stand out:

1 Students of all types of colleges expected that in their personal development college would help them toward self-actualization—

capability in making their own decisions, in expressing themselves, and in forming their own values — and achievement of a wider range of knowledge and greater tolerance of other people and other ideas than they had at entrance. Graduates of all types of college also thought it more important that college concentrate on producing well-rounded students rather than on the specifics of scientific method, scholarship, creativity, or mastery of the great ideas and the facts about the great minds of history. Other studies (College and University Environment Scale surveys, for example) suggest greater disparity of aims among entering students of different types of colleges than the NORC alumni showed between alumni of different types of college; so these data suggest that some "socialization" toward a general ideal of liberal education defined by these specifics may have taken place.

2   The reported expectations of independent and Protestant college graduates differ in particulars from the national averages and from one another, but not markedly. For example, Protestant college graduates placed more than typical emphasis of other groups on preparation for marriage, forming personal values, and tolerance for others. The private independent college graduates placed more emphasis than others on developing objectivity and acquiring a broad knowledge of the arts and sciences. Both groups of private college graduates were much less concerned than the average group about job training or career preparation. This is in keeping with the less frequent concern expressed by them for a stable and secure future in getting a job. The independent college group most often thought it important to form lasting friendships at college.

3   This picture of expectations gains importance when coupled with the alumni perceptions of the actual effects of college upon students. The independent college graduates most often reported actual gains in what we have called self-actualization — capability to think and express themselves and form their own values and goals for life, increased tolerance for others, and broadened knowledge. Protestant college alumni report more frequently a gain in knowledge of others, but less frequently in knowledge of themselves. As they saw it, they had learned to get along with others, to be more tolerant, and to form lasting friendships. More often than the average group, they reported acquiring a broad knowledge and learning to express themselves. However, they saw themselves less often than average for all alumni as having formed their own

values and goals for life. In view of the priority this last item has in both Protestant college aims and in student expectations, it suggests a need on the part of those colleges for fundamental reappraisal, not of their aims, but of their strategy for pursuing them. This type of success or failure, as perceived by alumni, seems to have influenced their later feelings about the college experience and may explain why the independent college graduates, more often than any others, claimed a continuing attachment to their college and desire to have their children attend it, even though they had often never revisited. Protestant college alumni were beset more frequently than average with mixed feelings about their alma mater.

4 There appear to be connections between the preceding data and alumni attitudes about career. On some points no major differences appear in the reported postcollege activities and interests and the expectations and experiences reported from the college days. For example, the number of children wanted, the number of books owned, and the number of different jobs held seem unaffected by type of college of origin. The independent college alumnus did not usually expect marriage preparation from college; and he married later, more often had a spouse who was also a college graduate though seldom from his own college, and more often than others expected to get more satisfaction in life from his career than from his family. Also, he did not expect to learn in college practical, effective ways of helping people, but had more often participated in volunteer service projects and considered the opportunity to be helpful to society a very important consideration in the selection of job or career. Coupling these data with the fact that he more often than normal went into law, medicine, business, and social science careers and, less frequently than Protestant college graduates, into education, indicates a different concept of "helping others" than is held by alumni of other types of colleges.

5 Although no group among those sampled had a sharp picture of the priorities in general educational aims of their own college faculty and administration, the independent and Protestant college graduates were somewhat more aware of what those priorities had actually been. The independent college graduates selected as official priorities (as distinct from their own personal ones) the production of well-rounded students, the development of objectivity about themselves and in their beliefs, and the cultivation of intellect. Protestant college graduates also recognized the production

of well-rounded graduates as an official aim and saw that training for careers had not held such priority, but they did not recognize the development of character of students as the priority one would have expected.

In comparison to the private college alumni perceptions of official aims, those of the entire sample of alumni present a picture that is highly undifferentiated, or perhaps even confused. That is, most aims averaged out to be seen as of "medium importance" to the faculty and administration, with the positive and negative responses on each item almost balancing each other out.

This lack of perceived clarity of emphasis may be of most critical importance for the productivity of a college. Perhaps the college did not, itself, set clear priorities; perhaps it merely failed to convey its priorities to students; perhaps it had different priorities for different subpopulations of students. In any case the impact of the college upon its students may be strongly affected by a lack of understanding or agreement on their part concerning what is expected of them, whether or not they themselves also share this expectation.

6   Most striking of the data from the alumni were the outright ratings which they gave their colleges. Alumni of independent colleges (not Protestant) for the most often rated their colleges excellent in caliber of classroom teaching, curriculum and course offerings, student housing, caliber of fellow students, knowledge and professional standing of faculty, and personal contacts with faculty. Particularly outstanding were the ratings on classroom teaching and on the knowledgeability and professional standing of faculty. Facilities and opportunities for research were most often thought poor by Protestant and independent college alumni (as compared with the total sample), while the average college graduate thought personal contacts with faculty poor (in contrast with the perception of both Protestant and independent college graduates). Related to these satisfactions are the additional, unusually frequent reports by Protestant and independent college graduates that there had been a sense of community and student participation at college and the fact that these graduates less often feel estranged from the "typical student" now at their colleges. The independent college and Protestant college alumni also more often than normal thought there had been intellectual stimulation; and the independent college graduates, that they had had a chance to gain an understanding of themselves and society. An interesting bit of negative feedback,

that may relate to the sense of community and support, is the shared perception of Protestant and independent college graduates that the rules at their college had been too restrictive.

7 In the types of professions they seek and the characteristics they consider most important in selecting careers, the independent college graduates indicate a greater than average concern with being autonomous and self-directed. They are more eager to assume leadership, more anxious to be free of supervision, more confident that they will make money, and more often than normal plan to be self-employed. They are, in this sense, more success-oriented. More had sought opportunities for advancement, though not in the sense of having a stable future or steady and modest pace of advancement, and more had sought opportunities to be original and creative. A greater than normal percentage of these independent college graduates were already working 50 hours a week or more on the job.

The Protestant college graduates in this study placed greater than average importance on being helpful to others and to society. More frequently than other groups, they found employment at colleges and universities and, more often than independent college graduates, were at work in primary and secondary school systems. Less often than independent college alumni, the Protestant college alumni sought to make money, to be free of supervision, and to have opportunity for advancement. They wanted variety in their work, but were not as often concerned as their independent college counterparts for more responsibility, autonomy ("control over what I do"), or challenge.

8 The religious and political views of the NORC alumni sample present complex differences among the types of colleges. In religious affiliation, independent college alumni were, more often than those of other colleges, Jewish, Presbyterian, or Episcopalian; while the Protestant college graduates were more often Methodist, Lutheran, or Presbyterian. Both independent and Protestant colleges had fewer Roman Catholic students, proportionately, than the average college. In politics, the private college graduates were more often Republican than average for all colleges; the Protestant college alumni were more often conservative than the independent college graduates, and the independents were more often liberal. Somewhat more independent college graduates than Protestant college alumni saw themselves as part of the "New Left."

Respecting "student power," independent college graduates

felt strongly that students should have the right to participate in decisions on the organization of the curriculum, but most did not favor such voice for students on faculty tenure, on what is taught in specific courses, on admissions standards, or on tuition and fees. Somewhat more often than others, the independent college alumni thought that students should be allowed to protest, to participate in politics, and to make their own rules on student behavior on campus and about political activities off campus; but they thought it not the college's responsibility to see that students did not break the law. The Protestant college graduates supported college responsibility for preventing law violation by students less than did independent college graduates, but agreed that students should make their own rules on their behavior and that the college should not prevent student participation in politics. The Protestant college graduates less often supported a student role in the making of decisions (tenure, course content, admissions, fees) usually made by faculty and administration. Opinion among both types of private college graduates was more than ordinarily divided on the question of whether they would approve their children's participation in antiwar protests. Most disapproved. But, interestingly enough, most of them favored such a part in civil rights demonstrations and considered student protests a healthy sign for America.

Both types of private college graduates favored state and federal provision of money for college education without governmental regulation. These alumni considered personal freedom an important factor in the choice of a college and, less often than average, thought good career preparation in college was important in this choice. A greater percentage expressed the preference that their children attend colleges of less than 1,000 students. While the Protestant college graduates showed no extraordinary interest in the college's providing a good religious education, they did display more frequent concern that the faculty and administration devote concentrated efforts toward the personal development of the student. Independent college graduates were the least concerned with this point.

Stern's Studies of Campus Cultures The ACE survey and the NORC alumni survey provide grounds for thinking that different types of colleges actually differ as cultural environments. This notion is further supported by the findings of George Stern of Syracuse University. Combining data from his earlier work with data from the Campus Governance Program, he found significant differences among the "culture scores" of different colleges and universities.[3] The culture scores are based upon a composite function reflecting both the campus environment and personality characteristics of the student body. Speculating that the nature of the environment and the mix of peers with whom students interact are two of the major factors affecting their learning, I believe that these cultural differences are an important element of the "resources" which affect capability for excellence.

Stern classified the campus cultures he found in five groups:

1 *Collegiate:* emphasizes play; close policing of behavior (low dignity accorded to students); a low press for academic achievement; social form received some stress, but academic organization little; students friendly and self-assertive

2 *Vocational:* a strong vocational press consisting of practicality, puritanism, deference, orderliness, and adaptiveness

3 *Protective:* high in supervisory closeness; high scores on group life, social form, academic organization, and self-expression; students scored low on self-assertion, but high on closeness, timidity, submissiveness, orderliness, and sensuousness

4 *Intellectual:* high intellectual interests and aspiration; characteristically favoring self-expression, vocational interests, and formal academic achievement

5 *Expressive:* low on vocational climate, non–work oriented, and nonconforming; students with nonapplied interests and disinclined toward orderliness; an aesthetic, gregarious, and nonpractical culture

For the samples studied, Stern found denominational schools as a type far into the protective domain and business administration programs at large universities into the collegiate. The other types of campuses studied reflected more nearly equal elements of the different cultural types, but elite independent liberal arts colleges fell between the expressive and the intellectual areas. Teacher-training programs ranged across the protective, vocational, and

---

[3] The Campus Governance Program of the American Association for Higher Education (1966–1970) made use of a preinterview questionnaire, the activities index, the college characteristics index, and interviews with faculty, students, and administrators on 19 campuses. The program was supported by a grant from the Kettering Foundation. Its findings are reported in Keeton (1971).

collegiate cultures, depending upon the type of school they were in. Engineering programs fell between the protective and the intellectual areas, closer to the former (Stern, 1970, fig. 73b).

In his samples, Stern found women teacher-training and university programs more collegiate than corresponding male groups, not because the women were more collegiate in orientation, but because of the press of their institutional environments. Someone apparently thought that young women needed a collegiate environment! On the other hand, among the independent liberal arts colleges, those for women were more expressive than those for men. Stern (1970) found considerable diversity among students, regardless of the school they attended.

In the Campus Governance Program, faculty, students, and administrators in each college were asked to check what they perceived as problems of their campus. Later, interviewers visited the campuses and inquired about both the reported problems and the ways in which they were met. The average number of problems reported per respondent was significantly greater on public four-year campuses than in private colleges, and greater on private college campuses than at community colleges. Analysis suggests that this difference is better explained by cultural differences among the types of campuses, than by the supposition that the difference is one of the number or severity of the problems.

In the Campus Governance Program data, Stern found significant differences between academic majors. When the sample was classified by type of control (public versus private), the public institutions were more collegiate than the private; and the women's private school sample was more expressive than the men's. The male private school sample of institutions shows no trends in any particular direction among the Stern vectors.

Throughout these data, according to Stern, student characteristics seem somewhat less significant in establishing the cultural type than does the press of the institution itself.

Stern also found significant subcultural differences within the same institution in a separate study on his own campus (Syracuse University). In this study, both the personalities of the students and the differences in environmental events appear to affect the subcultural differences, though the variation between student personalities in the subcultures is greater than the variation between the environments. It also appears that extremes of characteristics among a few students in a subculture may affect the character of the whole subculture markedly, whether these minorities represent an ideal toward which the campus strives or an unwelcome deviance.

Finally, Stern investigated the degree of dispersion and the sources of dispersion within campuses on the variables he was examining. The relative dispersion of scores around the group mean may be viewed as a measure of cultural heterogeneity of an institution. In the effort to create a productive campus one might hypothesize, as I have said, that the combination of relatively congenial subcultures with the challenge of an interacting and relatively heterogeneous campus could be highly productive. The campuses Stern studied showed relatively little heterogeneity in this sense.

The studies here reported suggest that the unique resources of private colleges go well beyond the physical and the financial. Their purposes, their faculty, their students, and the environments they generate result in the formation of cultures which are unusually effective for learning.

4. Vignettes of Excellent Colleges

For our purpose of understanding what colleges have greatest potential for excellence in undergraduate liberal education, data of the types discussed in the last chapter suffer because they are highly abstract bits of information about complex learning environments. Because of the complexity of these environments and of the dynamics of learning, a college might contrive to develop many of the "stigmata" of excellence reported in such studies and still fail to produce a whole environment and process of learning that are highly productive. From this point of view, vignettes of whole college environments, though in a sense much more subjective than hard data, offer a more reliable picture of a college's strength and a more valid notion of what really makes for this strength. In the course of the present study, my colleagues and I visited and participated in workshops with representatives of some 40 colleges, other than the 12 reported in much greater detail in our earlier study on the future of liberal arts colleges. In that study, the emphasis was upon understanding the diversity among strong colleges. Among the excellent colleges depicted were Oberlin, Amherst, and Earlham; others we subsequently visited were Knox College and the Claremont Colleges in California. Particular attention was given to Scripps, Harvey Mudd, and Sarah Lawrence colleges. Documents have also been studied on Bowdoin, Mills, and similar colleges. A sense of the variety and utility of these institutions can be gained from the profiles that follow.

MILLS COLLEGE Mills College is a privately endowed, nonsectarian school for women. Located in Oakland, California, it was moved in 1871 from Benicia where it was founded in 1852 as the Young Ladies' Seminary. It has deliberately remained small, the thinking being that ideas and intellectual enthusiasms are most readily transmitted in an "intimate" atmosphere. Mills attracts students of high academic potential with high-income family backgrounds. In a recent entering class 69 percent had been in a scholastic honor society in high school; 35.5 percent had been president of a student organization; 33.9 percent had published original writing. (Average SAT scores for 1966 entrants were 600 V, 580 M.) In academic interests, 35 percent declared an initial interest in humanities, 22 percent chose art as a probable career, and 30 percent wished to enter the social sciences. Sixty-three percent of their fathers had taken graduate or postgraduate degrees. Predictably, half of the students sampled expressed no concern over financing their education. The income of 40 percent of their parents was over $20,000 per year; and for 21.6 percent, over $30,000 per year. Data indicate that 94.6 percent felt that Mills students were of high academic caliber; 90.1 percent felt that Mills built poise; and 76 percent confirmed that classes were informal and that campus life was warm and intimate.

Students at Mills are influential in eliciting changes in college programs. Recently the Black Students Union there made several demands, all of which were met to their satisfaction (adding a black professor and a black counselor, a course in Afro-American studies, etc.). Mills has long emphasized having a diverse representation of religions, cultures, and nationalities and has recently pressed the recruiting of motivated Negro students of impoverished backgrounds who normally would not have been accepted there.

Thus in its mix of students and in their ability, cultural background, motivation, and expectations, Mills meets a number of the primary conditions conducive to a high degree of growth and learning among students. Moreover, Mills provides unusually fine resources for the offerings it makes and has been able to recruit faculty with both high conventional credentials and high commitment to Mills goals. Clearly its climate is congenial to productivity.

BOWDOIN COLLEGE

Bowdoin College in Brunswick, Maine, has defined its mission as the provision of a good liberal arts education in the conservative tradition—the education of the "total man" with the ultimate aim of "serving the common good."

This mission is outlined in six specific objectives of the college:

1 The cultivation and improvement of the students' mental powers

2 Breeding habits of mind—the moral as well as intellectual qualities of intellectual poise, disinterested opinion, and patient courage to pursue goals out of choice, not compulsion

3 Development of individual talent

4 Training of whole men—not allowing students to limit their interests

5 Giving students a knowledge of world culture

6 Serving the common good through its educated students

Bowdoin holds that this traditional definition of education can best be filled by a private college which devotes itself to these goals. It is selective in admissions (average SAT, 605 V and 632 M in 1966). However, there is a tension between the goals of developing the whole man and the students' expressed desires for more career preparation. The president mentioned this tension in a recent annual report and said the college would have to find ways to satisfy student desires without jeopardizing the objectives of the college. Implementing the conservative orientation of the faculty and the students, there have recently been major curricular changes —changes seen not as something new, but rather as a "better way" of doing things.

KNOX COLLEGE Knox College presents less congruity of objectives and intellectual style than Mills, Oberlin, or Earlham. Students were predominantly Midwestern in origin and, though well above average, not as strong in aptitudes or academic background as the students of Mills, Oberlin, and Earlham. Yet the faculty were among the best paid in the country (AAUP ratings of straight A and of AA in some categories), with credentials to match. In class the press for outstanding student work was high. A college with Knox's mix of students and faculty may actually have greater impact upon the students it does get, than one with greater congruity of ability and background between faculty and students. Much more precise research would be required for an assessment of this impact. Knox is characterized by a strong drive for institutional improvement and, in this sense, seemed more actively "on the make" than colleges striving only to "maintain their excellence."

CLAREMONT COLLEGES Scripps and Harvey Mudd of the Claremont Colleges present an excellent example of the possibilities of diversity within a closely cooperating consortium. The whole group of colleges has one of the outstanding libraries in the nation. The sophistication of business services available at relatively nominal costs is another distinction of the group. Yet in size, intimacy, and distinctiveness of mission the component colleges differ significantly. Parker Lichtenstein and Robert MacDowell, who visited in the winter of 1969, noted that both Scripps and Harvey Mudd provided exceptional resources and faculty and were highly selective in their admissions. Harvey Mudd is almost entirely a male school, and Scripps is a women's college; yet being adjacent, they reflect the atmosphere of a coeducational institution. At the same time they keep intact distinctive characteristics of a men's or women's college in internal student organizations, dormitory life, and class atmosphere. (Cross-registration is encouraged in certain cases.) In view of data from the Campus Governance Program and other sources, the focus of Scripps upon the social sciences and humanities and of Harvey Mudd upon the natural sciences provides another source of fruitful diversity. Scripps, at the time of our visit, was experiencing turmoil over demands for black studies; the turmoil seemed to hinge on recent unresolved student power issues. Scripps appears to have recently developed, in place of a finishing school atmosphere for affluent young women, a new look, that of a sharply inquisitive, highly intellectual place in search of contemporary relevance. (Average freshman SAT scores were 612 V and 572 M in 1966.) Its students reflect the grace of its earlier tradition, yet at the same time display the brightness and intellectual concerns of those at colleges with a stronger scholarly reputation. Harvey Mudd students, either because of natural priorities of interest or the press of their scientific studies, seemed more conventional in their interests and technical in their orientation. Freshmen SAT scores ranged from 480 to 780 on Verbal Aptitude, but from 600 to 800 on Mathematical Aptitude. The contrast between them and a public technical university's students, however, would probably reveal the former's breadth in background, interests, and social attitudes to be somewhat stronger.

SARAH LAWRENCE COLLEGE In my visit to Sarah Lawrence, I was particularly interested in the fate of its don-donnée system in a time of financial pressures. Sarah Lawrence is one of fewer than half a dozen colleges in the country which has done the most to individualize learning. Less affluent than most colleges of similarly high reputation, it nevertheless has held firmly to a pattern of one don concentrating his advising and tutoring efforts on seven students. The degree requirements give maximum weight to the judgment of this don and to his responses to the individual girl's intellectual and artistic interests. Though flirting with the idea of becoming coeducational,

Sarah Lawrence still has a distinctly women's campus climate coupled with strong intellectual press and a predominance of the arts and humanities. (Students come with average SAT-Verbal scores of 650, SAT-Math of 580—1966 data.) I sensed a rising, but not militant, articulation of a need for improvement in that the emphasis upon individualization of studies be complemented by stronger group academic efforts. (The college has, of course, had lecture-discussion and seminar classes all along.) Location and the ethos of Sarah Lawrence have helped the college draw strong faculty, and its smallness and the vigor of its leadership have contributed to a clarity of mission uncommon among even private colleges.

HAZARDS OF UNIQUENESS The hazards for private colleges which strive for a unique form of excellence are many: An urgent need at a given time may gain public recognition and be served later by publicly subsidized institutions. The need may be so well served that it ceases to be a continuing need. Or, the unique task may be well chosen but poorly managed. A promising beginning may be smothered by a hostile environment or by internal campus forces which work against it (e.g., the priorities of professors or the latent needs of students). Sometimes, also, the unique institution caters to an ill-chosen purpose (e.g., resistance to racial equality).

The colleges just described—from Mills to Sarah Lawrence—have avoided these pitfalls and survived public competition. They are clearly outstanding options in liberal education. Other colleges, not as outstanding as these, nevertheless, offer alternatives which should interest legislators, trustees, and college staffs who seek to understand the opportunities and the hazards of doing a unique service.

Norwich University offers a liberal arts program with a philosophic commitment to "the military way of life." Norwich, founded in 1819, the first private military college in the United States, provides a practical, as well as theoretical, education. It is the acknowledged father of the Reserve Officers Training Corps. Norwich contributed nearly 1,700 officers to the armed forces during World War II, including 16 generals and 1 admiral. Like the colleges already mentioned, Norwich views its obligation to educate as extending beyond the classroom. It provides physical, religious, and moral training as well. Admission is contingent upon presentation of "evidence of physical ability to undertake military training leading to a commission upon graduation" in the Army Reserve Corps (*Norwich University Record,* 1968, p. 23). SAT scores range from 500 to 599 in both verbal and mathematical aptitude.

In his military training as a member of the Corps of Cadets, the student learns obedience to authority and in turn learns to exercise properly constituted authority over others. By accepting responsibility as a way of life, he in turn becomes responsible. He gains self-confidence and ability to lead by training and practice in leadership. In addition, he is taught the duties and obligations of a patriotic citizen (*Profile of Norwich,* 1965, p. 5).

On the practical side Norwich offers such curricula as civil, electrical, and mechanical engineering; business administration; chemistry; and teacher education.

The Norwich concept of "responsibility as a way of life" might be defined differently at Bennington or Berkeley. But, as in the case among competing religious orientations, the key to America's achieving the needed qualities in its array of colleges must lie, not in uniform requirements, but in a social process in which students, contributors, trustees, foundations, public agencies, and other constituencies exercise choices, the aggregate of which determines the fate of the individual institution. With the evolution of world order and national defense, the function which Norwich has had may vanish or undergo transformation. Its long existence as a private institution performing a function closely linked to national defense is testimony to the surprising forms feasible in a dual public-private system of education.

Two of the institutions we have studied attempt, under private auspices, to center particularly upon the needs of the immediate community. They are private community colleges offering a four-year undergraduate program of studies. One began as a junior college, the other as a Bible college. Both then changed auspices and functions. The change was prompted in Little Rock University by a public university's termination of its extension offerings in the capital city. This move prompted a group of civic leaders to obtain a donation of land and to conduct a drive for funds to expand the private junior college into an institution which would offer, primarily for local students, "the opportunity for maximum self-development not only in preparation for chosen professions and vocations but also for general education, by which is meant an understanding of the various fields of knowledge and of the discipline of learning. It also seeks to stimulate community interest in academic pursuits." Finally, the catalog says, the university "expects its graduates to be responsible and loyal citizens who grow steadily in outlook, adjust to desirable changes, and achieve continued self-discipline toward a better moral, spiritual and physical way of life." Clearly in this case "maximum self-development" for the students is not the same process, nor has it the same results, as at Bowdoin or Scripps; yet the aspiration for impact in relation to a widely shared core of objectives of liberal education is present, with local color added to fit local needs.

In the case of the Bible college turned denominational liberal arts college, which in turn became an independent liberal arts college, the aim was service to "the average student" of its Midwestern state, who might not be accepted at private institutions elsewhere. The recent growth of public education in the state makes this mission in itself less distinctive than it once was, so the question as to the viability and need for the college turns upon the manner and adequacy with which it achieves this end. Its curriculum now includes a number of preprofessional programs such as teacher education, medical technology, and mortuary science. Many students are drawn from the fourth and fifth quintiles of their high school classes. Low attrition rate enables the college to sustain the desired enrollment, and this rate of attrition is doubtlessly related to the low tuition, possibly also to patience as to rate of achievement. In 1967 the college exceeded its salary budget in an attempt to recruit qualified faculty, but six positions, including that of dean of women, were unfilled. It is doubtful whether such colleges can ultimately survive public competition, because it seems likely that students and parents will find the cost prohibitive. The case cited, however, does not represent a truly outstanding management effort.

In some cases the improvement of options is not so much a matter of implementation of some new ideology, either educational or religious, as it is the difficult matter of social invention of better ways of achieving objectives that appear in statements on higher education. Take, for example, the utterly orthodox aspiration to individualize instruction. There is a great hue and cry for clearing the undergraduate colleges of the universities of the depersonalization which is said to have set in as a consequence of growth. It is commonly thought that a key obstacle to such individualization of instruction is cost. There are, however, methods of individualizing instruction that would actually save on costs. However, these methods run up against public and professional biases. In its design for a new college at Columbia, Maryland, Antioch College set up a venture which is by no means approved by all of its faculty. Permission to try the design was available because Antioch is trying the idea that pluralism within its own midst is desirable and can only be achieved by permitting ventures about which the majority has substantial reservations. The venture at Columbia uses substantial numbers of students as staff. It has only rented facilities, owns no dormitories, draws upon the Washington-Baltimore area for atypical proportions of part-time faculty, and enrolls atypical proportions of older students and of students of racial minorities. Typical departments and divisions are missing at Antioch Columbia. Instead there are the centers for human ecology, arts and the community, social research and action, and development of personal resources. The traditional Antioch alternation of work and study is replaced with a predominant emphasis upon concurrent work and study. Great stress is placed upon engagement with the surrounding community in both work and study. If approval of each and all of these changes by a faculty-student majority had been essential to the experiment, it could not possibly have been tried.

This philosophy of permitting sponsorship of innovation which the majority views with skepticism is open to public institutions as well as to private ones. However, public institutions are rarely in a position to pioneer ventures which offend the majority convictions so deeply. Monteith College at Wayne State University is one of those rarities (Riesman, Gusfield, & Gamson, 1970). Monteith mixed an urban, largely immigrant-derived student population with a curriculum derived from Hutchins' University of Chicago and a faculty bent upon close student-faculty relations. The venture threatened Wayne State's sense of professionalism and academic standards. The Monteith life-styles were also abrasive in their context. Monteith has therefore been under constant threat to its survival. Such a college may survive but not thrive.

On the other hand, the experimental college at the University of Michigan has many of the characteristics of an outstanding private liberal arts college. The sponsorship it gained probably derives, in part, from the fact that the University of Michigan, itself, displays unusual autonomy and quality among public institutions. It is unclear whether ventures such as those at the University of

California's Santa Cruz and Irvine campuses will produce distinctive gains in effectiveness in undergraduate liberal education since the campuses lack the degree of autonomy enjoyed by Michigan. There is also the question of whether a program will erode into normalcy or become extinct in certain environments through a lack of faculty interest. The Tussman program at the University of California, Berkeley, for instance, has been dropped from the curriculum for the time being, not because of opposition from the board of regents or the public, but largely because of a lack of faculty interest.

With reference to the provision of socially needed but unpopular ventures, the times may be changing, and large universities may become able to support small ventures which earlier could not have survived in a public context. A substantial sharing of authority and governance with students could contribute to such programs. I am convinced that various reforms in higher education which are centered around the changing of curricular content are far less fundamental in their implications for the improvement of higher education than approaches which make a major shift in the distribution of authority within a college. Public institutions, particularly large public universities under the control of state regents, are peculiarly at a disadvantage in pioneering educational innovations. Public systems in which there is the type of autonomy enjoyed at the University of Michigan have a better chance of being responsive to these needs. This is true also of state systems in which the authority of the statewide board of regents is restricted to quite general questions, with local boards or administrations given a larger hand in governance. The reforms under way in Canada illustrate a nationwide system which seems better adapted to respond to innovative needs.

Many discussions of colleges suffer from a tendency to imagine that society will be best served if we are altogether explicit and clear about objectives and functions of colleges. Colleges have many latent functions not recognized by professors or deans. Judson Jerome (1970) makes this point:

To be sure, the professoriate tells us repeatedly that the university is not for everyone — and that we are mistaken in trying to make it so. Some say we should kick out of our colleges all but the real students, the gentlemen scholars, who share the professors' commitment to work in the academic disciplines. That would be a good solution except for the fact that most of such professors would promptly be out of a job, and the few who remained would not have the laboratories, libraries and salaries they conceive of as necessary for their work.

Imagine such a purge of our institutions. Cull those Barzun calls the mandarins, who are not there to learn but to qualify. Cull the anti-intellectuals, the militants, the experience-seekers, the group-gropers and T-groupers, the great washed masses who are none of these but who are content to be herded along, not wanting to rock the boat, not wanting to risk their degrees and jobs and deferments. Cull the sycophants, the hustlers, the socialites, the influence peddlers and seekers, the red-necks. Cull the lost flower children, searching for their identity, confused about their goals, drifting in fuzzy clouds of introspection. Cull, of course, the athletes, the flashy frat boys, the sex hounds, the drug cult, the pranksters, the collegiate rah-rah crowd. Cull the adolescent rebels who are chronically opposed to all authority because they cannot stand their parents. Cull women. Cull draftdodgers. Cull the inadequately prepared, the products of poor schools, the stupid, the lazy, the disadvantaged, the spoiled. Cull blacks who are not willing to accept the standards and goals of our educational institutions. Cull the vocationally oriented, the teachers back for summer school who only want a raise. Cull dilettantes, the bored, the culture-seekers. Cull the childish, not mature enough to be away from home. On one end of the log remains Mark Hopkins. On the other end is a mirror.

One quite genuine, even though in many quarters unwelcome, function of colleges today is that of refuge, if not of sanctuary. College has been a sanctuary from the long arm of General Hershey's draft. On some campuses a drug subculture flourishes with implied protection from police that is matched only by Mafia enclaves. Where else but on the campus is experimentation, not just in intellectual phantasies but in political, emotional, sensual, and sexual behavior, tolerated under such respectable cover?

Nor is the campus only a refuge for youth. It is an "out" for parents at wits' end about uncontrollable and unmanageable youth. College is a convenient, socially approved way to get away from home. Getting away from home may be escape from parental domination; it may be a break with the oppression of one adolescent peer culture and a search for a more congenial one. It may be the ticket into the big, bad world, a place to make the contacts to be used in later life, a way to rise above the parents' social class or to drop out of an unwanted membership in class privilege.

Colleges serve as marketplaces for business and industry whose recruiters, unless driven away on moral issues about their involvement with war, come to campus every winter and spring. College is the auctioneer's block where professional athletic promoters resupply their aging stalwarts from among the college stars.

Mothers send their daughters to some colleges to "find a nice young man" to marry, and the college has the task of making the young woman into a more acceptable marriage partner than she otherwise would be. A small number of women's colleges are clearly finishing schools which survive economically on this continuing utility. In some cases they are also havens from racial integration. It is instructive to study catalog copy to discern how these two messages—we are a marriage mart, and we protect you from integration—are conveyed under cover of educational and legal sanction.

Less concealed, but often understated, is the increasing function of liberal arts colleges as prep schools for graduate study and professional training.

In recommending to colleges a greater self-awareness of their distinctive functions, I do not mean to say that all trace of unacknowledged latent functions should be wiped out. In some cases (as in that of preserving racial segregation) the moral fiber and health of the nation require that a housecleaning occur. In others it might be healthier to be open about the utility of the college. In any case, candor and self-awareness can contribute to the recognition and implementation of functions that benefit the institution and our society.

5. Public Policy for a Dual System

Earlier it was recommended that private colleges prepare to accept in the next decade an increase in enrollment which will, nevertheless, allow for a small decline in the proportion of private to public college enrollments of between 5 and 8 percent. This may seem a strange recommendation at a time when many observers are prophesying the demise of private higher education. But I am convinced that most private colleges are viable and, with greater sustenance, can become still more productive. Higher education as a whole will also be more effective and more efficiently provided if a dual system of private and public colleges is fostered under conditions favorable to a healthy competition in the public service. That competition can help to eliminate the private colleges which do not deserve to survive.

Harold Hodgkinson (1970, p. 8) suggests that alarm about the end of private colleges is premature. It may be that anachronistic patterns of expansion continue in colleges which are going from bad to worse, but, on the whole, private colleges—whether vintage or new—are capable of growth and utility. However, this requires change in the sources and magnitude of their support and in the management of their expenses.

Between 1941 and 1945 both private and public institutions of higher education decreased in number, but between 1955 and 1966 both increased—public from 652 to 806 different institutions, or a 23.6 percent gain; private from 1,203 to 1,446, or a 20.2 percent gain. Overall, the proportion of public to private institutions changed from 67 percent private in 1941 to 64 percent in 1966, with not over 4 percent variation during the 25-year span (ibid.). As reported elsewhere, during this same period, the proportion of enrollments shifted from 51 percent private to only 33 percent. The number of students of the individual institutions changed drastically. In 1947, public institutions averaged about twice the size of private (2,102 to 1,039), but in 1966 this ratio had become more nearly 3.6:1 (4,911 to 1,374).

This same study by Hodgkinson showed no change in the proportion of sectarian to nonsectarian institutions in the period 1941 to 1966: 40 percent were sectarian in both 1941 and 1966. This may change, as many church-controlled institutions, especially Catholic ones, reorganize their boards of trustees to become religiously-oriented institutions not controlled by the church organization itself.

Although the proportion of coeducational institutions to men's or women's increased (overall gains of 4 men's, 18 women's, 414 co-ed), there were slight gains even in the men's and women's institutions. For this period at least, the widespread impression that men's or women's colleges were vanishing is not warranted.

Also during this 25-year period since 1941, there was a net increase of 104 institutions granting the M.A., almost all of them moving from the status of previously offering the B.A. as the highest degree.

Hodgkinson's studies show, in the period 1949–1966, 118 four-year colleges that dropped out of existence—fewer than the number of "less than B.A." institutions dropping out (165), and more than other categories (49 with M.A. as terminal, for example). At the same time 272 new B.A.-granting colleges opened (72 granting the M.A.), while 510 new junior colleges (granting less than the B.A.) opened.

TABLE 3
Number of private colleges by highest level of offering

Level of offering	Private independent	Private, Protestant	Private, Roman Catholic
2 but less than 4 years beyond 12th grade	100	77	80
Bachelor's and/or first professional degree	224*	283*	201
Master's and/or second professional degree	126	93	88
Doctor of Philosophy or equivalent degree	81	29	22
Other	14	4	0
TOTALS	545	486	391

*Colleges referred to in this study come primarily from these two groups.

SOURCE: Figures from *Education Directory, Part 3, Higher Education, 1967–68,* 1968.

Hodgkinson suggests a vertical mobility pattern in which prestige and likelihood of survival complement increasingly advanced curricular offerings. Unless the decade of the sixties shows a change of trend, however, one cannot from these data support a theory that disaster confronts the private colleges.

In the country as a whole, admissions directors are reporting a slackening or a drop in applications to private colleges. Enrollments, nevertheless, continue to rise numerically, though not in proportion to total enrollment of combined public and private colleges.

When these data are disaggregated and the cases of individual colleges are examined, a quite different picture emerges. Some private colleges are experiencing a sharp increase in rate of applications and are planning confidently to grow in size without creating unmanageable problems of gap between tuition income and total expense. Other private colleges are barely keeping pace in applications, but have found substantial continuing external support. A few are steadfastly committed to a highly selective policy on admissions, holding total enrollment steady, increasing the costs per student at an even more rapid rate than merely keeping competitive would require. They are quite content to serve a declining proportion of the college population as long as those are served exceedingly well.

Because of (1) their heavy dependency upon student-derived income and (2) the variety of demand among prospective collegians, different colleges will opt for different responses to the quantitative

Private, with other religious affiliation	*Proprietary (profit-making)*	*Total*
3	23	283
20	6	734
4	1	312
8	0	140
1	1	20
36	31	1,489

Control	Number of institutions
Private, independent	545
Private, Protestant	486
Private, Roman Catholic	391
Private, with other religious affiliation	36
Proprietary (profit making)	31
Total private	1,489
Total public	1,000
TOTAL ALL INSTITUTIONS	2,489

TABLE 4 Institutions of higher education by type of control, 1967–68

SOURCE: Figures from *Education Directory, Part 3, Higher Education, 1967–68,* 1968.

needs of higher education, but all will face hard financial challenges. How can financing be achieved?

A typical college, undertaking to carry its share, might increase its enrollment 4 percent per year, and its costs would rise 5 percent to 7 percent per year as it sought to sustain the quality of its effort. The net result would be an aggregate increase of 55.4 percent to 70.6 percent in the annual operating budget within five years. As most colleges now keep accounts, the annual operating costs do not include capital outlays for buildings, unusual development efforts in program or finance, and other long-term investments in the institution's capabilities. How, if at all, can private colleges cope with cost increases of this magnitude?

This will require the collaboration of state and federal policymakers and administration with college leaders. The Carnegie Commission's earlier recommendations (1968, p. 15) concerning the main forms of support for higher education represent an appropriate first set of priorities for this collaboration. These forms of support include: (1) grants and loans to individual students to move toward the goal of equal educational opportunity, (2) support to institutions to meet increased costs of expanding enrollment and to strengthen areas of particular national concern, and (3) extension of support for research, construction, and certain special programs.[1]

Within this framework of support, the following policies are recommended as appropriate to further a dual private-public system

[1] In weighing options about what to recommend in the following points, I have had the use of a survey of college presidents' opinions by Ronald Wolk. See Appendix C for details.

of higher education most likely to foster both equal opportunity and the continuous improvement of the quality of higher education's services.

1   Legislators should view higher education, at both public and private institutions, as a joint investment by individual students and the general public. Public policy and practice should reflect this outlook. Legislators would then base appropriations upon estimates of the proper sharing arrangement for the two.

2   Legislation and administrative priorities in government, both federal and state, should focus upon enabling qualified students to afford the higher education of their choice without delays based upon difficulties in financing, rather than upon directly providing all the needed education under public auspices to those who cannot afford private education under current patterns of support.

3   Federal and state effort should give priority, not to meeting all current costs of any particular subset of institutions of higher education (such as community colleges or four-year state colleges), but to capitalization of the needed quality, types, and amount of educational services in the system of higher education as a whole.

4   Within limits the federal government can serve more needy students by subsidizing their loans or by encouraging combination grant-and-subsidized-loan packages of financial aid rather than by focusing exclusively upon grants to the neediest or funneling all possible needy students to state-supported institutions.

5   Policy should aim at substantially increasing borrowing and earning possibilities for students in such a manner that a parity is achieved between costs of public and private institutions. Thus a student would be able to obtain the best buy possible in his particular field of interest. Tuition charges should not completely drain a student's financial resources by creating a situation in

TABLE 5 *Earned degrees conferred 1967–68 in United States institutions of higher education*	*Control of institution*	*Bachelor's*	*Master's*	*Doctor's*
	All colleges	636,863	177,150	23,091
	Private colleges only	243,156	64,526	8,934
	Percentage of degrees conferred by private institutions	38.18	36.42	38.69

SOURCE: Figures from Hooper & Chandler, 1969.

which he is completely reliant upon tuition reductions, available grants, and personal earnings.

6   Charges to students should enable colleges to achieve a balance of income and expenditures on an annual basis if possible and, at longest, on a triennial basis. To make this objective practical, colleges should be expected, as a matter of public policy, to do true cost accounting on a program basis and to insist that "each tub stand on its own bottom": Over the long run (with five to ten years as an outer limit) each program should generate income equal to its expenses. One effect would be elimination of programs for which there is not enough demand to make them economically sound. A corollary effect is decentralization in the management of colleges, with accountability linked much more directly to educational productivity than now.

7   Public policy should encourage substantial efforts to achieve gains in the productivity of teaching and administrative personnel and to apply a substantial part of such gains to arresting the costs of· educational services, rather than plowing all gains into improvement of services.

8   While investing in any improvement of programs which, upon hard analysis, offer genuine promise, an institution should rely for long-range solvency upon the growth of tuition income and upon income automatically linked to it (e.g., federal grants to the institution per student graduated or serviced), rather than upon unpredictable private and public funding.

WHO SHOULD PAY FOR HIGHER EDUCATION?   *What should students pay?* Private colleges are more heavily dependent upon income from student tuitions than are either private universities or public colleges and universities. Howard Bowen (1968, p. 7) argues that students bear three-fourths to seven-eighths of the true costs of their higher education. Since this condition acts to retard progress in filling society's needs for highly educated people, Bowen contends that a redistribution of these costs is required if we are to do significantly better as a society.

William G. Bowen, though he makes a lower estimate of the proportion of cost borne by students, presents data to show that, even on Howard Bowen's terms, the investment in higher education is one of the most economically productive a student could make. William Bowen is, then, less alarmed by the prospect of continuing rises in tuitions and in the tuition gap between private and public universities, particularly in view of the fact that the noneconomic benefits of a higher education are recognized by alumni as substantial. In an earlier study of policy on the sharing of costs for Canadian universities, a strong case was made for a substantial participation by the federal taxation system in meeting the costs of higher education for all qualified students.

Theodore W. Schultz (1968, p. 327–347) has provided a sophisticated definition of the capital-forming functions of education in the discovery of talent, in instruction, and in research. He confirms the view that earnings foregone by students are well over half of the real economic costs of the human capital formation provided by higher education. He also defines an approach to planning and financing higher education built upon analysis of its rate of return as an investment. He argues that resources for higher education should be allocated in accordance with two tests: (1) that of economic efficiency, and (2) that of social policy on inequality in the distribution of personal income.

If economic efficiency of the whole system of higher education is one of the goals that future managers of private colleges are to serve, and if students and their parents can contribute to this goal by having a greater choice of which colleges students enter, as the Bowens and Schultz hold, then the conditions essential to this effect would include (1) students' acquiring optimal information and (2) an efficient capital market serving students.

The social policy that is to govern public sharing of higher-education costs is appropriately a controversial matter. It seems clear that much of the social benefit of a highly educated citizenry will be lost in the immediate decade, unless there is substantial public assistance for students who would not or could not otherwise choose and obtain the particular form of higher education most appropriate for them. During this period there is an urgent need for analysis of such issues as that of the social value added by higher education.

Federal Support and Private College Solvency The financing of private independent colleges, as distinguished from private independent universities, appears from federal government statistics to involve much greater dependence upon student-derived income and upon earnings from endowment investments: 75 percent as compared with 50 percent on student-derived income; 9 percent as compared with 6 percent on endowment income, as shown in the 1965–66 Higher Education General Information Survey (1967). These percentages are based upon combined income for education, auxiliary enterprises (housing and dining halls), and other institutional activity. The private universities get much more federal funding for research than do the private undergraduate colleges, as one would expect; and this help is largely concentrated in a handful of elite universities. Of the current funds from federal revenue that the private undergraduate colleges do get, only half goes for organized research; and this sum is 80 percent of the organized research revenue these colleges get. In a word, these colleges are proportionately much more concentrated upon teaching and caring for students than are even the private universities, not to speak of public universities. This relationship is also reflected in expenditure patterns.

Howard Bobren examined the outcome of financial operations (expense minus income) as disclosed in the HEGIS data and again found no case for doom to private institutions. For all private independent colleges, there was a surplus of 2.6 percent of the budget (as against only 1 percent for all independent higher education). This result occurs even though the colleges spent 54 percent more on student aid than they took in for that purpose: In short, part of their expense went toward subsidizing the student rather than paying for educational costs. The private colleges, as contrasted with private universities, broke even on organized research (a loss of 4 percent for all independent higher education, including colleges). Both private colleges and private higher education as a whole show profits on housing and food services (10 percent colleges, 11 percent overall), but these figures probably conceal a failure to charge against these services their appropriate share of overhead, amortization, and other costs. On other auxiliary enterprises, private colleges lost a net of 1 percent, while all private institutions made 5 percent.

Dr. Bobren found, however, that when his analysis took account of size of college a different story emerged. Colleges enrolling under 1,000 had a surplus of only 0.3 percent, while medium-sized colleges had only 0.7 percent surplus, but large colleges (5,000 to 10,000) had 4.3 percent surpluses and colleges over 10,000 had 14.5 percent surpluses.

As might be expected, private gifts and grants accounted for 63 percent of capital funds recepts (58 percent for all private higher education), of which 51 percent are for physical plant (54 percent for all private institutions). Endowment took the bulk of the rest

(41 percent in colleges and in all private institutions), and future endowment, in the form of annuity and living trust funds, was next in importance (7 percent colleges, 4 percent all private institutions). The larger institutions get proportionately more capital funds from the federal government, less from private gifts and grants.

Only in loans do private colleges obtain their primary resources from governmental sources. In 1965–66, private colleges obtained 42 percent of their physical-plant loans from the federal government, 16 percent from state government. With respect to student loan funds, 97 percent came from the federal government (as was also the case with private universities).

In summary, the dependence of private colleges upon federal assistance has been primarily in grants and loans for capital purposes. As costs per student rise and the number of needy students rises, the dependence upon federal help for loan capital for student loans will become more critical unless powerful and effective incentives are provided to induce private lending for this purpose. In addition, the gap between student ability and willingness to pay the total bill for education in private colleges will force the colleges to seek tuition grants for needy students or institutional grants to reduce the net costs to be met by student-derived income.

COST VERSUS OPPORTUNITY   It is a familiar concept in commercial marketing that an entrepreneur profits more by improving his product or service and raising his prices than by restraining improvement in the effort to drive down or restrain prices. Because of the high costs of higher education, the limited ability of many qualified students to pay, and the limited philanthropic and public resources available to fill this gap, college administrators have fallen into a pattern of holding costs below an optimal level for educational performance in an effort to accommodate deserving students. I believe that this stance will be increasingly anachronistic from both the perspective of the college's own solvency and that of public service. Colleges should price their services at their true net cost and provide means by which students can earn or borrow to meet the difference between their own available funds for higher education and the charges they must absorb.

For most private colleges this policy would represent (1) greater emphasis upon work assignments and loans than upon grants, and (2) greater emphasis upon study-related work as a source of student income. In the HEGIS data for 1965–66, for example, private colleges gave relatively more grants than did private universities, and relatively fewer work assignments and loans. Of their loan funds, moreover, private colleges got only 28 percent from the federal government, as against 38 percent for private higher educational institutions as a whole. This difference may be explained in part by the fact that graduate programs can obtain federal loan funds more readily than undergraduate, and students in graduate school may be more willing to borrow to complete their degrees than are undergraduates. (Figures on current outlays for loans are to be distinguished from those cited earlier about loan capital increments.)

Antioch College is attacking the problem of suppressing costs and enlarging opportunity through programs at its Graduate School of Education and its Columbia (Maryland) Undergraduate Center. The primary problem is not recruitment (applications and registrations exceed the program's capacity), but rather: (1) obtaining from banks and other capital sources sufficient money to meet students' needs and (2) arresting and reversing an earlier trend toward upper-income enrollments.

In the case of Antioch College, the work-and-study tradition provides two financing options for students and for the college. One involves arranging work experiences close to and concurrently with academic studies in a pattern that enables the student to optimize income within a pattern of work compatible with serious study. The other option is that the college may accept contracts for research and other services which it renders, not primarily for the contract income, but for the work-and-learning opportunities which the contracts provide "in-house." The danger here to be avoided is that of becoming "contract happy" and taking on jobs that do not give adequate intellectual stimulation to students or that do not represent an opportunity for faculty advancement. The contracts also must be handled in a manner congruent with the institution's priorities and not as a simple response to market demand. The effect of contracts properly managed is to decrease the net cost of the student's education, to increase the supply of jobs most appropriate to the concurrent and productive interplay of work and study, and to elevate the average earning per hour for students.

Antioch's Master of Arts in Teaching program has actually reversed the traditional pattern of college selection which results in a high incidence of affluent students. The proportion of students receiving loans or grants exceeds 69 percent and the proportion of ethnic minority students has risen from 7 percent to over 35 percent in the last four years.

Efforts of the kind being undertaken at Antioch are essential to adequate capitalization of student costs for tuition and living expenses. It may only be possible to achieve results on a large scale if the federal government is the primary guarantor.

INCREASING EFFICIENCY When faced with large financing problems, managers naturally seek to cut prices and costs or at least to arrest the rate of their rise. But, as I have pointed out, cutting prices (in the aggregate or in the gross amount per student) may not even serve the cause of increasing patronage. Cutting costs per student may be poor policy. The viability of private colleges will turn upon their service's being a best buy, a bargain for the money, not upon being cheap. This is not to rule out cutting costs where it can be done without loss of quality service. To be competitive in the market for students and for contracts for research and instructional services, an institution should first be in a position to render a service that cannot be as adequately rendered by others. In this case it may be legitimate to have abnormally high charges. For the type and quality of service rendered, a college should not make significantly greater outlays of dollars and talent than other competing institutions. This demands efficiency. Are there strategies that promise more than superficial gains in efficiency in undergraduate education? I think so, but they differ from the approaches most commonly emphasized today.

Faculty Output per Man-year A key barrier to prosperity of colleges is their failure to find ways to increase productivity per man-hour as labor and other costs rise. When we examine faculty-student ratios in particular colleges, however, we find radical variations among colleges of acknowledged high quality, from a 1 to 7 or 1 to 9 ratio in a few well-endowed institutions to a 1 to 19 ratio in a college such as Antioch. As a practicing administrator familiar with the myriad idiosyncrasies of professors and colleges which can interfere with a nice abstract theory such as the Ruml-Morrison formula for efficiency, I nevertheless believe that it is entirely feasible to achieve a 1 to 30 faculty-student ratio and still maintain an excellent instructional program.

A productive measure for increasing faculty output or "impact" per term or year is offered as illustration. It involves reducing the number of students a faculty member serves at one time, while increasing the total he serves per year. Work-study programs typically achieve this result, but it is possible by other means as well. Kalamazoo uses an "independent study quarter out of residence" and a period of study abroad. At Antioch, which is a classic user of this arrangement, students spend alternate quarters away from campus on jobs except in their last year (three quarters in residence). The result is a 1 to 19 budgetary ratio of faculty to students (i.e., 19 student tuitions per full-time equivalent faculty salary) at the same time that there will be only 13 students in residence to 1 full-time teacher on duty (faculty teach 3 quarters per year; students are in residence only 2 except in the last year). (Costs and efficiencies of work-study plans are analyzed in a recent paper by Morton Rauh [1970].) Research has repeatedly shown Antioch "overproductive" (Alexander Astin's term) of learning as variously measured, so that it cannot reasonably be claimed that this cost efficiency is obtained to the detriment of education. To be legitimate in terms of the aims of American education, this kind of instruction plan must serve not only to help the college make ends meet but also to advance its educational task.

Often the reaction to the proposal that others use a strategy such as this is that it is unique and, hence, not relevant elsewhere. This is unwarranted. The great majority of colleges today show interest in (1) the use of first-hand experience in interaction with study as a vehicle for deepening and accelerating learning and (2) the use of independent study tactics both to generate more scholarly attitudes and habits in students and to gain efficiency. Often the particular mechanisms used for these purposes are counterproductive. For example, independent study will be so defined and conducted that it requires even more faculty time per student for comparable learning outcomes than do seminars or regular classes. Even colleges which are committed to a considerable element of one-to-one interaction between faculty members and students will find that they can better achieve this if they conduct a substantial part of the processes of learning by methods requiring less faculty time than is typical today. In this connection, one of the colleges I visited, Sarah Lawrence, a model of individual learning, treats the don-donnée relationship as the keystone of its educational design. Students at Sarah Lawrence have begun to complain in substantial numbers about being too tightly controlled and restricted in this relationship, too isolated from the interactions they might have with peers, and constricted in pursuing their own intellectual interests.The dons, too, were discontent with what was perceived as an overemphasis upon one-to-one relationships in learning to the exclusion of one-to-many or many-to-many relationships. In response to this situation, I proposed a modified don plan which would involve the dons'training some upperclasswomen to supplement the dons' present seminars with additional peer-group learning sessions and with other one-to-one relations other than those of the don and donnée. The scheme would permit a 33 percent to 50 percent increase in students per don, overall, and effect a reduction of costs. It seems plausible to expect that the climate of learning would be as rich as, or richer than, at present.

A four-year program of experimentation with independent study at Antioch led some faculty and staff to conclude that the number of classroom contact hours between faculty members and students had, within a range of 33 to 50 percent less than conventional faculty-student contact hours, no measurable effect upon learning. Moreover, autonomy in study is fundamentally not a matter of mechanical arrangements, but of the attitudes and habits of inquiry of the participants. For example, a faculty member who is a reasonably clever manager can serve his students better than others with much less personal contact. This may seem contrary to what is generally considered the proper course of action in administering a liberal education. But if the faculty member is to elicit drive and initiative and independence of judgment among students, his excessive presence or his domination of the learning process (whether he is present or absent) can actually be counterproductive. Similarly if he is so hostile to ideas contrary to his own that under the guise of fostering controversy he beats down opposition, underplays the merits of opposing ideas, or uses his position to suppress genuine inquiry, his contribution, again, is counterproductive.

These considerations have led us in this study to search for vehicles of efficiency in learning. Universities often strive for this and fail. For example, the use of graduate teaching assistants as part of the teaching staff in which a senior professor and possibly others assist in conducting a course with large enrollment—a "differentiated staff"—serves to reduce costs. One such arrangement at a large university produces tuition income of $240,000 per year and expenditures of $80,000 for the graduate assistants, costs of the services of the faculty, and overhead costs. But the purpose here is to subsidize the graduate school. "Efficiency" is gained, but not in the sense of lowering the ratio of cost to benefit for freshman students. Cost per freshman is lowered, but so is the quality of instruction to freshmen. The saving in costs is reallocated to the graduate school for its research and other functions.

To achieve a true benefit to the undergraduate student with the differentiated staffing pattern, it is necessary to alter not just the practices of an individual teacher but the system of instruction.

A number of private colleges have found that undergraduate teaching assistants can be even more productive educationally than the typical graduate assistant in the large university. In the private colleges with long experience with such assistants, the assistantship is typically a reward for distinguished work as a student. The student takes the option in part because of its utility as a learning experience and often as a vehicle for exploring his interest in college teaching as a career. The average aptitude and background of students in the assistant role is superior. Normally the professor does not assume the degree of distance and noninvolvement in the total teaching that typify some university courses using graduate assistants. In some cases the undergraduate course using undergraduate teaching assistants also uses a preprofessional laboratory technician.

The key test of any arrangement for differentiation of staff is that of its using the highest paid staff for only those tasks which they alone can most efficiently perform. Superior equipment or supplementary staff can contribute to this effort. So also can the sharing of a service with other institutions or the use of the same activity for more than one educational purpose.

Keeton and Hilberry (1969, pp. 340–342) write:

The use of the same activity for more than one educational purpose is a familiar practice that could be much more widely applied. It may produce two or three benefits for little more than the price of one. Many colleges draw on public schools to provide practice teaching opportunities for undergraduates; or a college may set up a laboratory school to teach undergraduates, to train master's students in education, to do research on learning, and to provide schooling for children. . . . A theater that mixes workshop plays—student-produced and even student-written—amateur performances open to the public, and professional performances with supporting casts of students, faculty, and townspeople can fill a community's need for good drama and serve as a richer laboratory for instruction than a college could afford on its own. . . .

Frequently a college or university in a given geographical area will have a program in rare languages or in a costly branch of science, a program of field research in the social sciences, or some other rather specialized educational service by virtue of government or foundation support. This special program may be underused, since its purpose is to introduce opportunities hitherto missing and to develop interests in its subject. If other users are charged the full unsubsidized unit cost, the price may be prohibitive. But if, in the stages of developing cooperation, other institutions are charged only incremental costs, usage may increase until the unit cost becomes bearable, and the supplying institution may be in a better position to command able faculty and to provide strong supporting staff. At [some] colleges, this sort of sharing occurs most often within formal associations — sharing of specialized courses by Morehouse and other members of the Atlanta Center and by St. Thomas and St. Catherine, sharing of graduate teaching talent by Amherst and the Connecticut Valley group, sharing of foreign study centers, field stations, language programs, and off-campus research, study, and action projects by the Associated Colleges of the Midwest, the Great Lakes Colleges Association, and the Union for Research and Experimentation in Higher Education.

Within a college, improvements of program or additions to staff often occur with little synchronization or symbiosis among these developments. A computer may be installed because a progressive college should have a computer, but the training of programmers and the development of instructional uses that would make the computer of really substantial help may come about only as an afterthought. Sometimes financial support is proffered to colleges in a way that fosters this uneven and wasteful kind of development, as when the earmarking of the grant explicitly excludes uses that would "compromise" a pure research effort or some other special purpose. Sometimes the most productive and efficient collaboration in program development may be of a type that links unlikely partners — biology with philosophy rather than chemistry, research with public service rather than with graduate study, postdoctoral with undergraduate teaching rather than with graduate study, etc. We expect that in the future, colleges will be more ingenious in discovering symbiotic relations among people, programs, and institutions.

Colleges can and should be more ingenious in the creation of efficiencies. Antioch is currently undertaking a radical venture in the new city of Columbia, Maryland, starting with an initial 80 students. All student housing is provided by commercial lessors, with the result that the capitalization and management of some hundreds of thousands, and later millions, of dollars worth of student housing is handled by people who specialize in housing management. Similarly, office space and all other facilities used for administration and instruction are initially (and possibly permanently) built and managed by others for the college. Such an arrangement is similar to the more typical ones in management of food services, of housing, and of underused academic facilities such as auditoriums, libraries, and conference and workshop space.

A last and most difficult priority in the achievement of efficiency in college administration is that of continuous study of cost-benefit relationships within the college operations. Administrators often throw up their hands in despair when this suggestion is made, because they realize how elusive is the problem of assessing outcomes of education and how difficult it is to change the habits of academia. Yet there are some areas in which management can clearly be improved.

Research Costs The growth of organized research has been one of the main forces behind recent increases in university costs (W. G. Bowen, 1968, p. 6). Many private colleges aspiring to excellence of conventional scholarship are moving toward increased support of faculty research as an integral part of the "educational and general budget." While I think well of this trend, a college should refuse to take such costs as pure "add-on," without built-in efficiencies in its overall faculty-student ratio and instructional yield from program activity. Typically a university includes some research costs in its instructional budgets on the grounds that its professors must engage in research to keep abreast as teachers. I would suggest a policy that requires the use of student aides and assistants in this research or in some other way forces a substantial contribution of such work to educational yield for students; that is, a greater yield than an alternative investment of the same money elsewhere would produce. Typically some of the costs of graduate students' participation in research seep over into the undergraduate instruction budgets through fellowships for teaching and research. This offloading of costs from graduate study onto undergraduate should be avoided especially by colleges and departments that are not experienced in conducting graduate programs, because their lack of expertise can lead to bankruptcy.

Specialized Curricula

Universities tend, more often than colleges, to feel obliged to add courses and curricula for each major national need or intellectual development as it occurs. Such additions are expensive and tend to be associated not only with increase in total cost, but also with higher rates of cost per student. Private colleges striving for excellence should change curricula through substitution rather than sheer accretion; if this is done, the rate of cost increase will not be as substantial as a university's.

Mix of Students

Another cause of rising cost per student in universities is the higher proportion of graduate students enrolled. Since the costs are higher for them than, say, for freshmen, and since this trend appears to be continuing, university costs may move upward more rapidly than college costs. The same trends that increase graduate student growth also affect upper-class student enrollment growth. But private colleges are often undersupplied with upper-class students relative to the number of staff assigned to advanced courses and can absorb the increases still with less growth in cost per student than will apply to graduate schools. Private colleges often retain highly inefficient departmental faculties on the grounds that inadequately used special curricula are needed for balance in the program of liberal studies. For example, two neighboring colleges in the Midwest recently had six physics faculty members apiece, all highly qualified, with fewer than ten senior major students in physics per year in each of the two colleges. While physics could hardly be eliminated from their curricula, it is ridiculous for them both to sustain such an underused staff when joint operation could provide better service at greatly reduced cost. In other cases it is likely that the underused specialty should simply be eliminated and that students needing that service should either transfer elsewhere or obtain the service from a neighboring institution or from a larger university.

A number of private colleges are beginning to seek subpopulations of students from minority groups or students without the usual qualifications for study in those colleges. This is being done on the grounds that the mix of students is itself a major factor in learning. Frequently, however, such students can only be well served if staff is provided to cope with their special needs. In undertaking such ventures, a college should take a hard look at the relative cost-benefit relationships involved and should consider alternative options designed to get the same educational benefit. Sometimes the outcome of such study would be, not a resolution to forego the venture, but a decision to take a much larger group of the new type of student so that the required special staff can be efficiently employed.

Use of Technology

It is fashionable today to advocate the addition of equipment and facilities providing the newest wonders of technology. Claims often are that the new equipment will yield new efficiencies. Normally, gains in efficiency from use of improved technology are more readily achievable where the task to be performed is one of a large volume of operations and is one of the less complex and less changing activities of the college. Thus elementary instruction, skill training, information transmission and recovery, and similar tasks are likely to offer the best opportunities for efficiency, rather than more sophisticated intellectual tasks. The use of technological improvements generally produces an enrichment of services and activity, rather than a reduction of cost per student. Colleges should use consultants whose business is not to sell equipment, but to help the college achieve efficiency by its own definition of the wanted mix of improved services and arrested cost rises.

Institutional Design

The most neglected aspects of efficiency efforts within colleges are probably (1) the failure to focus upon the gains to be realized by eliciting student commitment, initiative, and energy in the learning experience and (2) the failure to design a strategy of instruction that would achieve an overall impact, rather than the splintered impact of individual professors upon individual students. These approaches are closely related, for the critical elements of design are the quality of learning achieved and the energy expended in achieving it, and these depend heavily upon student commitment to the college objectives and the energy they put into pursuing them.

I am convinced that most colleges do much too much for students which students could do better for themselves. The course of learning is excessively regimented. Provisions for housing, dining, studying, and even socializing are arranged and regulated for students who might better regulate these matters themselves. Clustering and grouping are preplanned according to notions which the faculty think ought to make sense for students, whereas the clusters and groups that would be most productive could better be worked out by students as part of their learning activity. All of this "doing for" students costs excessive faculty time and administrative effort; at the same time it precludes discovery of better ways and discourages the very initiative and responsibility which would be most productive of significant learning. Ventures by private colleges which are willing to risk unorthodox outcomes for the sake of greater student commitment to learning are likely to result in cost control—if this concern is also kept candidly open for student collaborative invention and effort.

DEVELOPING INCOME

Private colleges have for several years faced the discouraging prospect of having to obtain more and more funds to serve their present enrollments. These difficulties will grow as an effort is made to take a share of the nationwide increase of students and to provide better services.

Net Charges per Student

It will not help colleges to give away an increasing proportion of the tuition increase as grants or tuition reductions. W. G. Bowen (ibid., pp. 39–41) shows that in Chicago, Princeton, and Vanderbilt in the period 1962–1966, the net income from student fees increased much less than the gross charges per student (only $87 per student net income as compared with $404 per student gross charge increase). Of the three main causes for this difficulty, only one—an increased proportion of students from low-income families —applies to colleges that are not in or entering substantial graduate programs. Insofar as colleges move toward the graduate school pattern of subsidy to able low-income and other special groups of students, then, they will encounter problems in the effort to raise net income per student. I would recommend a contrary course; viz., that the *subsidy* of deserving and needy students is not the function of the educating institution per se, but is the responsibility of state and society. The college should, as far as possible, collect its entire charge; and the mechanisms for supporting persons who lack means or seek especially favorable terms of support should be distinct from those of managing the educational task. This is not to say that a college may not appropriately operate under the policy that wealthier students subsidize poorer ones, but, if so, this should be done by "overcharging" the one for any "undercharge" that is made to the other. Similarly, it is not to argue against giving the benefit of gifts and other net income to students by reducing the net charge. But here again the college's realization of a charge adequate to sustain its program should not be dependent upon uncertain gifts and other income.

A number of colleges have had considerable success in the past 15 years in increasing the proportion of student financial aid in the form of loans rather than grants. This change has the effect of enabling the college to raise charges as well as the percentage of charges that amount to net income. Colleges can strengthen the use of tuition for income production by developing means for students to borrow larger amounts under interest terms and repayment terms that are favorable.

Sophistication in Fund Raising   One factor in a predicted decline in proportion of income derived from private gifts in the next decade is increasing competition for the private gift dollars and the fact that most universities have in the past 10 to 15 years utilized a sophisticated and costly pattern of fund raising, one from which in many cases only modest improvements can now be expected. With rising taxes, continuing inflation, and incomes rising less rapidly than costs of higher education, the outlook for private gifts is less rosy than in the recent past, we are told. It is true that a few private colleges have matched the most sophisticated efforts in this respect. But the great bulk of private colleges have not made effective use of fund-raising techniques. Our case studies suggest that an appeal to a distinctive audience may be relevant not only in attracting students, but also in attracting private gifts.

By selective response of donors to a distinctive mission as a result of energetic presentation of need, one college met within eight years a budget increase from $200,000 to $2 million, with a growing margin of surplus per year and a rapid capital expansion. The college's own explanation was that "God has, in answer to prayer, faith and obedience, performed miracles beyond the capability of men."

Another college discovered that "most of the wills in which the University has been named were made during the lifetime of the founder . . . and the new friends we have been cultivating . . . are still alive." The growing longevity of men of good will is thus another frustration of the deserving college. Even so, this college expects gifts of $10 million within the decade just begun. Generally, income from endowment currently represents a declining proportion of college income because it has proved difficult to keep the corpus of endowment rising in proportion to the growth of enrollments, and the rates of return have not risen proportionately to meet inflation. Much attention has been given within the past five years to improving the yield from endowments (see, for example, the Yale University report on its plans). Small colleges can usually muster sophisticated investment counsel only if they band together or enter into a contract with a larger program. Nevertheless, a few small institutions have continued to succeed in achieving substantial increases in endowment, and a college should surely check its potential for such help rather than assume that the general condition necessarily fits its own case. One locally oriented private college has received a single bequest involving perpetual increments from the growing market value of a trust naming the college as sole benficiary. Thus far the trust has yielded more than $4 million.

Different colleges derive their primary gift support from different types of sources. This last-named locally oriented college gets its primary gift support from local businessmen and citizens who apparently see it almost as a community college in its utility to them and to the youth of the area. Mills College parlayed a Ford Foundation award of $2.2 million, which was to be tripled, into gift income of over $11.5 million, meeting half of a 10-year goal within three years. Generous alumni and wealthy friends help to make Mills secure. Still another private women's college on the East Coast recently received $1.7 million from friends to purchase and renovate a building. One hard-pressed new college had been more successful with capital gifts than with current operating expenses and had borrowed from its own capital funds to avoid payless paydays. This practice, once condemned out of hand by accreditors, is now viewed with less certainty by critics: *If* a college is solvent overall, if it has a sound plan for repayment, and if it will do better in the long run to borrow its own capital funds than to leave them in low-yielding investments and borrow at high interest rates, borrowing from endowment may be sanctioned. Thus Knox recently used some endowment funds for buildings.

In W. G. Bowen's study (1968), the declining proportion of college students likely to have or to achieve riches is expected to affect adversely the private giving for such institutions as Princeton and Chicago. For many private colleges the trend may be the reverse: Their alumni are part of a population group which is upwardly mobile; that is, they are not the selective, elite college drawing only upper-middle- and upper-class students, but a less affluent clientele. These alumni are likely to be, in the aggregate, better able to help in the future than in the past. But if, as the NORC data from alumni suggest, private independent college alumni feel that their alma maters are more deserving of support and of students than do the alumni of other colleges, this factor may also bear upon capability to sustain private gift support.

Reliance upon Foundation Giving

The prospective relative decline in foundation support for higher education reported by W. G. Bowen (1968) is likely to hurt graduate education more markedly than undergraduate. The extensive fellowship support from foundations to universities has been predominantly directed toward graduate studies. Also the proportion of budgets derived from foundation sources has been larger for universities, and the part of such help that was integral to the continuation of basic programs seems to have been less for undergraduate than for graduate programs. This does not mean that private colleges should expect substantial new help from foundations, but that, having had little help, they should feel its absence less than universities.

Auxiliary Enterprises

Knox College has undertaken the most daring ventures in auxiliary enterprises to produce income for the general operating budget. Knox has formed a separate corporation which acquires enterprises or generates them, and which manages them with a view to their net income's use for the benefit of Knox College. A highly sophisticated board of directors and strong managerial talent are responsible for the choice and conduct of these enterprises. To undertake this type of venture, it is essential that a college command such talent in both trustees and management. If the managers and trustees available to the college with these talents are too few, both to manage the college well and to manage the other enterprises well, the college should give first priority to the sound management of its educational enterprise. It is too early to assess the utility of these auxiliary arrangements. In the past an occasional college has been substantially assisted in endowment growth by ownership of business ventures or property (Wesleyan with educational publishing, for example), but other instititutions have, especially in the ownership of land and buildings, had difficulties in finance, in public relations, and in internal relations as a consequence of being landlords.

Managing Endowment for Income For most colleges income from endowment has recently been declining in relation to total income. A few have pioneered in the management of their endowment and endowmentlike funds in a way that gives high priority to the objectives of income improvement but lower priority to security of holdings and the increase of interest income. This type of management of endowment puts a heavier than usual proportion of endowment into stocks which promise to rise in market value, even though the percentage of interest and dividends is low. The increase in market value is treated as income, some of which is put back into endowment to keep it growing and to act as a reserve against market declines. But the balance of the increment in market value and interest is spent on current operations. The Ford Foundation has published a study on the legality of, and the conditions to be met, in using endowment this way. The 1969–1970 market decline points up the caution with which a college should approach the management of endowment.

In summary, provision of a better than average "buy" in educational services, and the marketing of this service at charges sufficient to support the services, should be the cornerstone of a college's income production. Other sources of income can then enhance the college's effort, and selection among them can be made on the basis of their yield relative to cost.

PUBLIC CAPITALIZATION OF COSTS Repeated reference has been made to the desirability of a nationwide program of loans to assist students to meet the costs of their own choice of college. The magnitude of capital necessary to fund such an effort nationwide is beyond the capability of private institutions, foundations, and individual donors, even in combination. For example, the Carnegie Commisssion (1968, p. 29) estimates that $2.5 billion would be needed in 1970–71, alone, to implement a version of this idea advanced by the Carnegie Commission; the need would be approximately $5 billion in 1976–77. Deferring this outlay, however, would result in a loss of national income and productivity larger than the cost of the proposed allocation. In addition, such delay compounds the inequities arising from unequal access to higher education today. The magnitude of the capital need is further increased by the demands that will arise for land, buildings, equipment, and other development resources as institutions of higher education attempt to serve sharply increasing numbers of students. By making substantial proportions of the needed funds available as loan capital, the federal government enters into a productive partnership with higher education to meet costs, which, if not met currently, will impede growth necessary to our educational system.

NEED FOR COMPETITIVE EFFORT

With costs rising both in the aggregate and on a per student basis, and with the capital needs of higher education straining the potential of even the federal government, it is urgent that waste, duplication, and inefficiency be held to a minimum. This cannot be done by fiat or by rule and regulation. This requires a system of higher education that has built-in, self-corrective mechanisms. Powerful among the possibilities is that of competition in a context in which clients have the information and the incentive to choose intelligently among options. Among the conditions necessary to achieve this result, the crucial ones are: (1) development of methods of identifying and making public the true costs per student of comparable services rendered at different institutions and (2) provision of the means for the prospective student and his parent to know what the student is getting for his money (a similar need exists for governmental and philanthropic support). Models both of true cost estimates and of vignettes of institutions and programs have already been developed in rudimentary form. Certainly practical difficulties lie in the way of making these models useful on a nationwide scale. But I see no way to escape confronting these difficulties if we are to sustain confidence in higher education as an investment.

One of the problems related to assessing costs and communicating qualitative differences among colleges is determing how public and private colleges should scale tuitions. In my view, legislatures should refrain from setting the charges which public colleges and universities make and confine their work to defining and allocating what they view as an appropriate share of public support. If the individual public college or university sets its own tuition and fees, it will then be in a position to choose its own distinctive level of service and to test its judgment in the marketplace. If legislatures begin to provide some per student allowance to private colleges, the gap between public and private tuitions may be held to a level that enhances competition and keeps the private colleges in business.

If the recommendations provided in this chapter are followed, it will be practical for private colleges to absorb the magnitude of increase in enrollment recommended earlier and to improve their educational programs as well.

6. *Achieving Quality*

This chapter concentrates on ways in which private colleges can encourage an array of campus cultures and serve a variety of purposes with high priority among national needs for higher education. The changes recommended to the colleges are: (1) a sharp realignment of rights, authority relationships, and procedures of accountability in college governance, (2) improvement of communications within the colleges, and (3) decentralization and differentiation of structures in the management of colleges.

REALIGNMENT OF AUTHORITY The productivity of the best of American institutions is a function of an unusual combining of liberty and mutuality. Freedom fosters initiative, energetic application to task, self-respect, and health of spirit. Mutuality reduces interference, injustice, and exploitation and furthers invention and fruitful collaboration. As society becomes more complex, it becomes more and more difficult to achieve maximum productivity, justice, and well-being by any means other than self-disciplined cooperation guided by shared respect and aspirations. Like our society, colleges are moving rapidly toward a complexity of task and makeup which demands the invention of modes of operation that are nonauthoritarian and collaborative. A college brings together, for purposes of furthering learning and maturity, people who differ sharply in experience, learning, maturity, and expertness. Yet a fruitful interaction among these people is essential to the work of the college.

In the Campus Governance Program of the American Association for Higher Education, a modest addition has been made to the data we have about perceived problems, sources of information, loci of ability to get things done, and needs and press within different campus cultures (Keeton, 1971). These data disclose a need for a redefinition of how a campus is to be well governed. There are several facets of this task: (1) Students, faculty, administrators, and trustees, when asked to name a campus's problems, differ markedly in their responses, and even within each of the groups there are often significant differences of perception as to the problems of primary concern. (2) There is often conflict over who should define the problems and assign priority to them. (3) There is, in addition, often disagreement within a campus regarding the standards, ideals, and objectives of "better governance and better administration." (4) At the same time different subgroups of different campuses converge in their perceptions and priorities in ways that are often unique to the specific campus.

The variety of these patterns of conflict and congruence of perceptions and judgments will multiply during the coming decade. Rather than "fight the trend" in the sense of refusing to acknowledge its force and relevance, college administrators and trustees should, where conflicts arise, begin with the working assumption that the conditions just mentioned should be accepted as a basis for improvements. These conditions should not be viewed as obstacles that have to be removed before order and good governance can be achieved.

What does it mean to redistribute authority in respect to purposes, ideals, standards, prerogatives, and the definition and resolution of problems? How can this realignment occur in a way that is compatible with the qualitative improvement of the college?

Shared authority is not authority granted on sufferance, as a sop for good behavior. At the same time, it is neither the sheer surrender of power by its present holders, nor the assumption of power by new ones, possibly students or faculty or particular pressure groups on campus. The tendency to read "sharing of authority" in this way may arise from the notion that power is like pie: If one party gets more, someone else gets less. Actually, in a human organization, collaborative effort can enable everyone to gain more of what he wants. If power is the capacity to gain an objective, then patterns of power-sharing that have this effect are the ones that should be used.

Using a collaborative style of authority-sharing does not mean putting an end to conflict. It means conducting the conflict within a frame of reference of determination to work together toward joint achievement. In the first substudy of the Campus Governance Program of the American Association for Higher Education, Arnold Weber and colleagues (1967) concluded that academic senates using faculty and administrative collaboration will be the most productive vehicle for academic governance. They also concluded, however, that on many campuses the senate structure can be used to cloak patterns of domination over faculty and students by administrators or statewide governing boards.

At private colleges, patterns of domination and internecine strife are less in evidence than in large universities, just as general campus unrest is less manifest. Alexander Astin of the ACE reported to the American Psychological Association a study (*College and University Bulletin,* 1969, pp. 1–5) of responses from 382 campuses about campus unrest:

> Apparently institutions which experienced more distruptive and violent protests than would be anticipated from the characteristics of their entering students tended to be universities, coeducational colleges, and public colleges.
>
> Institutions that had fewer protests than one would expect . . . tended to be four-year colleges, technical schools, liberal arts colleges, and private non-sectarian colleges and to have environments characterized by a high degree of concern for the individual student.

Unrest, Astin concluded, at least that of a disruptive or violent nature, is in part a response to a feeling that the welfare of the individual student is slighted.

Elaborating on "protest-prone" institutions, Astin characterized them as having "environments which were incohesive; moreover, students and faculty had little involvement in the class, students were not on warm, friendly terms with the instructor, and they were not verbally aggressive. . . ."

Not enough is known yet about the causes and cures of such disruption to assure any college administration that it can, with the best of competence and good will, wholly avoid disruption. Nevertheless, there are factors that reduce its likelihood—smallness, coherence of purpose among different component populations, concern for the individual student, and a style of governance in which conflict and disagreement can be accommodated within a framework of mutual cooperation.

IMPROVEMENT OF COMMUNI-CATIONS A key to fruitful changes lies in the realm of the informal relations among students, faculty, administrators, trustees, and others of the college community.

In the campus interviews of the American Association for Higher

Education's Campus Governance Program, it was found that on both public and private campuses, informal lines of communication and decision making differ from the formal. Formal and complex institutional organization normally accentuated the tensions centering around governance and compounded the difficulties of resolving problems among conflicting groups.

Informal communications often enhance collaboration. On some campuses we have found that presidents used periodic open houses or retreats with trustees to provide, not merely social acquaintance, but a regular opportunity for those not normally in contact with the president or trustees to convey information and to exert influence. Other administrators have used an "open-door policy" and managed to make it effective.

Informal communications permit people to develop trust and to exchange ideas, information, and attitudes so that their behavior becomes predictable and understandable. Trust, in this sense, does not mean agreement or compliance with the same concerns but rather respect for purpose and intent, and understanding by each of the bases for the others' acts. Informal communications can, of course, sharpen conflict and distrust. Often distrust is the fuel that electrifies "the campus grapevine." The point is not that informal communication offers a panacea but that it is a critical force in patterns of influence and must be among the vehicles given major attention in effective governance.

The preinterview questionnaire data of the Campus Governance Program repeatedly disclosed discrepancies between student, faculty, and administrator reports of problems. Students and faculty also sought out different "visible figures" on campus to "get information" and to "get things done." It would be useful for a college to take periodic surveys of working relationships so that policies and management might be based on awareness of these relationships.

DECENTRAL-IZATION AND DIFFERENTI-ATION Small private college campuses have shown greater than average flexibility in the past half decade in introducing new modes of effective communication and new mechanisms for faculty and student voice in governance. Although it is only possible at this point to hypothesize about these data, it seems likely that the larger a college and the more extended the steps of decision making, the more difficult it is to achieve a collaborative spirit in the things that matter to groups within the college. Relatively small primary groups with authority to decide matters of concern to themselves can more easily become collaborative because informal communication can be more economical, rapid, and expeditious than formal communication in dealing with accumulated grievances and distrust. The research of Likert and others in management of business and other organizations suggests a similar hypothesis. If this hypothesis is correct, then colleges would do well to explore patterns of decentralization which grant authority and rest accountability in subcolleges or subunits of government and management. Other factors, such as the personal needs of participants and their previous experience in governance, will, however, affect the capacity of the group to make effective use of decentralization.

Decentralization is a neglected alternative because faculty and administration normally insist upon prior checks which delay action. This prevents subunits from taking risks and suffering or enjoying the consequences of their own judgment. Checks often take the form of "channels" which must be pursued endlessly before action can occur; the stress upon following "channels" generates logrolling tactics. To avoid this result, colleges should consider using subunits which have the authority, though small, to grant the degree or to manage a whole program. To implement this idea requires the collaboration of other subunits, since a small unit cannot supply all of its own needed services. But if such a small unit is free to enter into contracts with other institutions for services which it cannot obtain within its own college, many of the barriers to internal cooperation can be dealt with effectively.

Decentralization requires the dispersion of leadership much more widely than is now common among the administrative staff, the faculty, and students. Most colleges are short of adequate leadership, as Pattillo and Mackenzie emphasized in their study (1968) of over 800 church-related colleges. One of the key reasons for this shortage of leadership is found in our conventional patterns of governance, which discourage initiative, entrench dependency, and limit the opportunities for experience in management essential to the development of a large corps of campus leaders. Decentralization thus implies the delegation of authority to unproven persons who will learn "the hard way" by making some costly mistakes while learning.

The problems of communications on campus are not essentially ones of technology, but of interest, attitude, and commitment. The very delegation of authority over significant decisions can have a salutary impact upon interests, attitudes, and commitments. Apathy often is the obverse of a sense of powerlessness, distrust, and disagreement with authority.

Decentralization will place upon colleges the demand for an investment in the training of those who will now undertake a greater part in governance and management. Some colleges are beginning to use leadership teams rather than traditional hierarchical administrative role-definitions. Such a team arrangement can fill complex demands for administrative work. It also gives members of the team needed rest, retraining, or changes of assignment without the disruption that "time away" creates in more conventional staffing. For such teams to develop effectively, however, the college must put time and money into training. With such training, a small group in charge of its own fate will frequently impose disciplines of economy and work which no central authority could.

Education is an enterprise in which "the exception is the rule" — individualization of instruction is at the very heart of the achievement of high quality. To gain efficiency in mass-producing individualized education, a campus must allow individuals who make up the student and faculty bodies to enlist the administrators in their intellectual causes. That is, the administrator should help them get resources and sponsorship without trying to control the performance of the tasks, other than to preserve and enhance the capability of the college to serve others.

The delegation of authority required for good campus governance reaches all the way to trusteeship. In his study of college and university trustees, Morton Rauh (1969, pp. 187–189) found that the trustees of private independent colleges are more disposed than average to leave critical decisions on faculty, curriculum, and student affairs to the president and his deputies and to the faculty. (Few showed much disposition yet to reach out to students with the offer of such responsibility.) As the functions of colleges grow in complexity, and as the changes needed to maintain and improve quality become more substantial, the importance of sound patterns of delegation of authority from trustees will increase. In this respect, the movement to add faculty and students to boards of trustees may be less important than a movement toward increasingly substantial delegation of authority with an accompanying increase of communications between trustees and campus personnel to assure the benefit of the diverse perspectives.

A TIME OF TRANSITION Ours is a time of transition in the role of private colleges in American higher education. It is a time in which they should shift from a passive responsibility for the equalization of educational opportunity. Private colleges, to meet this responsibility, cannot only arrest the rate of decline of the proportion of college students whom they serve. They must clarify their aims. They must have the courage to identify the variety of needs they can serve in higher education and to offer the resources that public authorities will demand of them. They must be prepared to initiate internal reforms required to provide diversity at reasonable cost and maintain quality of performance appropriate to the opportunity.

In making these recommendations for realignment of authority, improvement of informal communications, and use of decentralization to improve college governance and management, I do not mean to suggest that good results will be automatic or easy. The obstacles are formidable. Charters and bylaws often stand in the way. Some of the attitudes of trustees (cited by Rauh) and faculty (as illustrated in the Campus Governance Program data) combine with certain facts about student cultures (as in the Stern studies, 1970) to challenge the most competent and energetic reformers. Limitations of financial and other resources frustrate even those campuses in which these other factors are favorable. The need for reform, however, is urgent. Our knowledge of what is involved in achieving reform is rapidly growing. The time is therefore one of great opportunity.

7. Summary of Recommendations

To achieve the quality of services from institutions of higher education and the equality of access to them which the Carnegie Commission on Higher Education has recommended, this book recommends (1) a substantial increase in the volume and the variety of opportunities for higher education, with culling and refinement of programs to assure efficiency and responsiveness to changing social purposes and circumstances, (2) provision of increasing financial resources and greater efficiency in their use, and (3) a more sophisticated division of labor among institutions of higher education than we have today.

The task of private colleges in this recommended transformation of higher education is twofold: (1) to accept a share in the recommended increase of students and to do so on terms that are advantageous to taxpayers and to state governments and (2) to undertake and sustain ventures in qualitative achievement for which private colleges are peculiarly qualified. Some of these ventures, which are either already in existence or in need of being developed, will be rooted in a philosophical or religious perspective which is inappropriate or illegal for a state-supported college. Other ventures may be of types appropriate for both public and private colleges, but fitted to the particular private college because of its resources in people, tradition, distinctive control, financial resources, or other resources and circumstances.

To enable private colleges to perform the proposed task, leaders of public opinion and institutions' governing bodies should weigh the following recommendations for public policy:

1 Legislators should view higher education as a joint investment by individual students and the general public. Legislators would then base appropriations upon estimates of the proper sharing of costs for educational services of both public and private institutions.

2 Legislation and administrative priorities in government, both federal and state, should focus upon enabling qualified students to afford the higher education of their choice without delays based upon difficulties in financing, rather than upon directly providing all or most of the needed education under public auspices to those who cannot afford private education under current patterns of support.

3 Federal and state effort should give priority, not to meeting all current costs of any particular subset of institutions of higher education (such as community colleges or four-year state colleges), but to capitalization of the needed quality, types, and amount of educational services in the system of higher education as a whole. Within limits the federal government can serve more needy students by subsidizing their loans or by encouraging combination grant-and-subsidized-loan packages of financial aid than by focusing exclusively upon grants to the neediest or funneling all possible needy students to state-supported institutions.

4 Rather than try to control quality or enforce standards directly, federal and state efforts should be directed toward providing a high quality of education by offering the public and private colleges and universities incentives to compete with one another.

5 Policy should aim at substantally increasing borrowing and earning possibilities for students in such a manner that a parity is achieved between costs of public and private institutions. Thus a student would be able to obtain the best buy possible in his particular field of interest. Tuition charges should not completely drain a student's financial resources by creating a situation in which he is completely reliant upon tuition reductions, grants, and personal earnings.

6 Charges to students should enable colleges to achieve a balance of income and expenditures. The colleges should do true cost accounting on a program basis to facilitate elimination of economically and educationally unsound programs and to provide adequate and fair support to sound ones.

7 Public policy should encourage substantial efforts to achieve gains in the productivity of teaching and administration and to apply a part of such gains to the arrest of rising costs.

8 Colleges should rely for long-range solvency upon the growth of tuition income and upon assured forms of public support (such as

grants to the institution per student graduated or grants to students that follow automatically from need and qualification) rather than upon unpredictable private and public financing.

To implement the recommended growth in enrollment and improvements in quality of higher education, colleges should undertake substantial changes of internal government and management. These changes should include:

1   A sharp realignment of rights in the determination of college purposes, the definition of problems and of the priorities to be followed in their resolution, and the prerogatives of those who constitute the college (trustees, administrators, faculty, students, alumni, parents, and other publics)

2   An improvement of communications on campus, with particular stress upon the climate and mechanisms of informal communication

3   Division of labor and decentralization in the governance and management of colleges, with a view to increasing the capability of effective action by subcolleges or programs

These changes in government and management should reflect a climate enhancing, on one hand, the freedom of constituent groups within a college to pursue their objectives and, on the other hand, mutuality in the support which each group accords to others and to the college as a whole. This climate is most likely to develop where the patterns of power and influence pursued enhance the ability of different groups to achieve what they want, rather than emphasizing their tendencies to block and interfere with one another. This climate rests ultimately, then, upon a shared willingness to legitimize in governance the perceptions and judgments of the diverse individuals and groups who make up a college, whether these perceptions and judgments diverge or converge. This change of participation in campus governance is recommended as a means of achieving unity of purpose among constituencies, even when they otherwise conflict or diverge in philosophy and objectives.

Commentary

A task for private colleges multiplies into a series of tasks, some of them supplementary and clearly related, and others, to my mind, contradictory. Morris Keeton's analysis of the task or tasks provides a stimulus for all those concerned with plans for higher education, private or public: for college administrators and board members, a stimulus to look critically at their own institutions and their own experience; for faculty members interested in judging priorities, a stimulus to consider critically both expenditures and possible economies.

Keeton believes that the task of the private colleges as a group is to undertake a part of each of the two main services suggested by the Carnegie Commission's recommendation for quality and equality. Some of his proposals will be noted without much comment, not by way of summary but only to make clear that if these are not accepted, a further search of the complexities involved is not likely to be of significance.

The system of higher education should be a dual system, independent and public. In some institutions public education has, of course, considerable "private" support; Keeton would like to see independent education receive more public support. His reasons are naturally not for "handouts" to maintain life where life should not be maintained. He is himself convinced that private colleges are lusty and growing, and his reasons for giving them greater support are clearly stated. The first is financial: to prevent undue increase in cost to the taxpayer as the expected higher enrollments require more places, some of which could in Keeton's opinion be provided by many (but not all) of the independent colleges.[1] To allow for expansion in this way would, of course, require a quality in independent education that at least matched that in public education.

[1] Keeton's figures will not be referred to but only the general expectations.

Keeton goes further: His second reason for giving independent colleges greater public support is to improve the quality of the education by counting heavily on the freedoms the different kinds of independent colleges have. One of the most interesting parts of the book is the consideration of these freedoms. Another is his idea that competition among institutions should be stimulated, and that in the process quality will be improved.

The sources of public support for private colleges are considered to be available, and some of the difficulties they have presented, e.g., the church-state issue, are discussed briefly. I should like to have found more discussion of these issues. The difficulties, especially in terms of state as compared with federal funding, seem to me so serious that they require more concrete proposals before even the prospect of public support is counted on. Public support also introduces two difficulties both in relation to the recommendations of the Carnegie Commission on quality and equality and in relation to the Keeton proposals: By no stretch of the imagination has public support reached the levels required for the hoped-for increase in quality or equality in higher education, and second, its delays—often at the present level of support disastrous to institutions—would have to be somehow reduced, or the deep troughs eliminated, before institutions could plan as surely on public commitments as some of them now plan on what Keeton occasionally refers to as the uncertain gifts and bequests from private sources.

A particular kind of public support seen as fundamental to the task as a whole is a rapidly expanding loan program. The loan dollars are, of course, cheap dollars in themselves, for the return over time is good, but loan dollars in so far as they increase the number of students also require some sort of cost-of-education supplement to the institution, whether from endowment income and gifts or from public funds, and as enrollment increases, even when major steps are taken toward maximum use of buildings, additional monies are required, as either grants or loans, for buildings.

Subsidies to the needy and deserving student are frequently part of an institution's budget, and Keeton recommends that they should not be; that, instead, they should be the responsibility of the state and of society more generally. He takes a further step in recommending that the institution should collect its entire cost. On this matter, which is still hotly debated, Keeton's position is that colleges should use every kind of support they can find, but that they should not be dependent on "uncertain gifts and other income" (p. 74). All students would then come closer to paying full costs, the poorer students through greatly expanded programs of grants and loans, and the wealthier students through family income.

But Keeton by no means concentrates only on matters of funding. He is interested in the many (and, he thinks, growing number of) variations among independent institutions, and he has studied intensively a small number of specific institutions. From a review of the backgrounds he concludes that colleges have had a "reluctant response to external pressures for reform" rather than a pattern of active leadership (p. 12). He would certainly not have found colleges developing apart from the society in which they were embedded, but it seems to me that he gives a number of examples of active leadership.

He recommends the pluralism of the colleges, reflecting the pluralism of the society—diversity ranging all the way from the religious to the new "radical" studies. Those concerned with planning for private colleges, whether from boards or faculties, will be particularly interested in these views, and his suggestions for "radical" studies should not be written off as a departure from reason in the direction of emotion, or any other dichotomy, but rather considered in a broad context of the interest in pluralism, and also in relation to his idea that students are increasingly transferring from one institution to another for a term or a year, and could well benefit from an environment very different from the one they had first chosen.

Pluralism includes not only differences in religious or philosophical perspective, but also differences in the characteristics of students or supporters and different innovations which may be risky or unpopular. Examples are given of a wider range of each type of difference than most persons concerned with college planning could readily find. One aspect of Keeton's view of pluralism should be noted directly, the view that the independent development of a particular philosophy or type is probably the best development. He grants that the particular philosophy or type may be accommodated within a large university, for example, by having students live in a religious house while they attend a university, but he argues for the separate development of a college with a particular philosophy or clientele. He questions whether "black studies" will contribute in the university framework of all studies what could be contributed independently, on the theory that in "every sound college education . . . the *Weltanschauung* itself should also be at times the object of scrutiny and doubt (p. 19)." He notes, as basic to the theory, Kenneth Boulding's view that "A major problem of the next century will be the preservation of subcultures within the "superculture" of a complex, highly organized world" (p. 21).

In terms of change of new ventures, Keeton is convinced "that various reforms in higher education which are centered around the changing of curricular content are far less fundamental in their implications for the improvement of higher education than approaches which make a major shift in the distribution of authority within a college" (p. 51). Even during the time required for his studies and their publication, it has certainly been clear that student participation, with or without advisers, has introduced many changes in the "liberal arts" curriculum. That these changes will continue is much less clear, partly because some of them, once introduced, have not been well supported by students and partly because their funding has been on an ad hoc basis, usually as additions to, rather than as substitutes for, earlier work, and always in the midst of controversy both within the faculty and within the student group.

One of Keeton's views is that colleges in general do too much for students and should rely more on student initiative, true independence in their work (and so a saving of faculty time), and far greater freedom in planning their lives. He does not note, as has been noted so often recently, that the greater freedom students have, the more extensive staff time often seems required.

Change and new ventures we know to be found not only in private colleges. Keeton seems to take a dim view of the extent to which public institutions can introduce innovations, but he also recognizes that times may be changing, and he cites a few of the important innovations recently made in them.

Competition among private colleges and between private and public institutions Keeton views as an indirect way of improving the quality of programs. With students paying something like full costs, and being well supported financially when they need financial support, the students will theoretically be free to judge quality and choose accordingly. Keeton also argues for cooperation and interinstitutional arrangements, and "the transformation" which he sees as possible in higher education if his recommendations are followed depends on both competition and cooperation.

References

Association of Independent California Colleges and Universities: *Financing of Independent Higher Education in California, A Summary,* Los Angeles, 1968.

Bowen, Howard: *The Finance of Higher Education,* Carnegie Commission on Higher Education, McGraw-Hill Book Company, New York, 1968

Bowen, W. G.: *The Economics of the Major Private Universities,* McGraw-Hill Book Company, New York, 1968.

Carnegie Commission on Higher Education: *Quality and Equality: New Levels of Federal Responsibility for Higher Education,* McGraw-Hill Book Company, New York, 1968.

College and University Bulletin, vol. 23, no. 1, American Association for Higher Education, October 1, 1969.

Coordinating Board of the Texas College and University System: *Pluralism and Partnership: The Case for the Dual System of Higher Education,* Austin, Texas, 1968.

Digest of Educational Statistics, U.S. Office of Education, Washington, D.C., 1969.

Educational Directory, Part 3, Higher Education, 1967–68, U.S. Office of Education, Washington, D.C., 1968.

Educational Policies Commission: *Higher Education in a Decade of Decision,* U.S. Office of Education, Washington, D.C., 1957.

Fletcher, Robert S.: *A History of Oberlin College from Its Foundation Through the Civil War,* vols. 1 and 2, Oberlin College, Oberlin, Ohio, 1943.

Hatch, Louis C.: *The History of Bowdoin College,* Loring, Short, & Harmon, Portland, Maine, 1927.

Higher Education General Information Survey, U.S. Office of Education, Washington, D.C., 1967.

Hodgkinson, Harold: *Institutions in Transition,* Carnegie Commission on Higher Education, Berkeley, 1970.

Hooper, Mary Evans, and Marjorie O. Chandler: *Earned Degrees Conferred, Part A, Summary Data, 1967–68,* U.S. Office of Education, Washington, D.C., 1969.

Jerome, Judson: *Culture Out of Anarchy,* Herder & Herder, New York, 1970, pp. 100–111.

Joint Economic Committee: *Economic Indicators, August,* U.S. Government Printing Office, Washington, D.C., 1969.

Keeton, Morris: *Shared Authority on Campus,* American Association for Higher Education, Washington, D.C., 1971.

Keeton, Morris, and Conrad Hilberry: *Struggle and Promise: A Future for Colleges,* McGraw-Hill Book Company, New York, 1969.

Kerr, Clark: "New Challenges to the College and University," in Kermit Gordon (ed.), *Agenda for the Nation,* The Brookings Institution, Washington, D.C., 1968.

Knapp, R. H., and H. B. Goodrich: *Origins of American Scientists,* University of Chicago Press, Chicago, 1952.

McGrath, Earl (ed.): *Universal Higher Education,* McGraw-Hill Book Company, New York, 1966.

National Academy of Sciences: *Doctorate Recipients from United States Universities, 1958–1966,* Publication 1489, Washington, D.C., 1967.

Norwich University Record, Norwich University, Northfield, Vermont, May, 1968.

Pattillo, Manning, Jr., and Donald M. Mackenzie: *Church Sponsored Higher Education in the United States,* Report of the Danforth Commission, American Council on Education, Washington, D.C., 1968.

Profile of Norwich University, Norwich University, Northfield, Vermont, 1965.

Rauh, Morton: *The Financial Advantages of Work-Study Plans,* Antioch College, Yellow Springs, Ohio, June, 1970. (Mimeographed.)

Rauh, Morton: *The Trusteeship of Colleges and Universities,* McGraw-Hill Book Company, New York, 1969.

Riesman, David, Joseph Gusfield, and Zelda Gamson: *Academic Values and Mass Education,* Doubleday & Company, Inc., Garden City, New York, 1970.

Rudolph, Frederick: *The American College and University: A History,* Vintage Books, Random House, Inc., New York, 1962.

Schmidt, George P.: *The Liberal Arts College,* Rutgers University Press, New Brunswick, 1957.

Schultz, Theodore W.: "Resources for Higher Education: An Economist's View," reprinted by the Carnegie Commission on Higher Education from *The Journal of Political Economy,* vol. 76, no. 3, May–June, 1968.

Science Research Associates: *Who Goes Where to College?,* Chicago, 1965.

Stern, George G. : *People in Context,* John Wiley & Sons, Inc. , New York, 1970.

Weber, Arnold, et al.: *Faculty Participation in Academic Governance,* American Association for Higher Education, Washington, D.C. 1967.

Woody, Thomas: *A History of Women's Education in the United States,* vols. 1 and 2, The Science Press, New York, N.Y., and Lancaster, Pennsylvania, 1929.

Appendix A: The ACE Summaries of Data on Entering Freshmen, Fall, 1967

In this report on the data from the American Council of Education Office of Research we are dealing with three categories of schools: large liberal arts colleges (enrollments of over 5,000), small liberal arts colleges (under 5,000), and Protestant (visible) colleges. The respective numbers of respondents are (approximate, since not all respondents answered all questions) 3,178; 15,562; and 11,709.

Since the N's are so large, inspections of the data used a 3 percentage point difference as being meaningful or important. We later decided to look most closely at those categories where 5 percentage point differences were noted. Some mentions were made of items which seemed related to these but which did not meet the 5 percentage point criterion.

We compared the norms for our three categories of institutions with the national norms, which also include Protestant (invisible), large and small public colleges, parochial colleges other than Protestant, technical and science schools, Negro colleges, and so on.

This analysis deals with only the "total" entrants rather than the breakdowns to male-female percentages—except for ages of entrants, which were done by sex as well as by total, and except for items on which response by sex differs significantly from the totals.

Independent Liberal Arts, Small (under 5,000)

Alfred University, Main Campus

Amherst College

Bates College

Bennington College

Berea College

Bowdoin College

Briarcliff College

Carleton College

Chatham College

Claremont Men's College

Colby College

College of Charleston

Connecticut College

Dartmouth College

Fisk University

Gallaudet College

George Williams College

Grinnell College

Hamilton College

Harvey Mudd College

Hollins College

Marietta College

Marlboro College

Middlebury College

Mills College

Morris Harvey College

Mount Holyoke College

Oberlin College

Pitzer College

Pomona College

Reed College

Rockford College

Rollins College, Main Campus

Scripps College

Springfield College

Stephens College

Swarthmore College

Sweet Briar College

Trinity College

Union College

University of Tampa

Vassar College

Washington College

Washington and Lee University

Wellesley College

Wesleyan University

Western New England College

Wheaton College (Massachusetts)

Whitman College

Williams College

Windham College

Independent Liberal Arts, Large (over 5,000)

Adelphi University, Main Campus

Bradley University

Monmouth College (New Jersey)

Pace College, Main Campus

Rider College

Tulane University of Louisiana

University of Hartford

Protestant (Visible)

Allegheny College

Augsburg College

Austin College

Beloit College

Calvin College

Carroll College (Wisconsin)

Concordia College, Moorhead

DePauw University

Dickinson College

Earlham College

Emory and Henry College

Franklin and Marshall College

Gettysburg College

Guilford College

Hamline University

Haverford College

Lake Forest College

Lebanon Valley College

Lindenwood College

MacMurray College

Mary Baldwin College

Occidental College

Randolph Macon Woman's College

University of Redlands

Valparaiso University

Wesleyan College

Wittenberg University

Wofford College

	Large (%)	Small (%)	Protestant (visible) (%)	National (%)
Age—totals				
17 or younger	7*	6	5	4
18	81*	76	83†	77
19	11*	12	11*	14
20+	1	5	1	3
Ages—males				
17 or younger	5	5	4	4
18	79†	70*	81†	73
19	15	17	14*	17
20+	2*	8	2*	6
Ages—females				
17 or younger	10*	8	6	6
18	84	82	86*	82
19	5†	8	8	10
20+	1	2	1	3
Average grade in high school				
A—, A, or A+	17*	20†	22†	13
B—, B, or B +	56	55	62†	55
C or C+	26†	15†	16†	31
D	0	1	0	1
Secondary school achievement				
President of an organization	25*	29†	30†	22
High rating—state music contest	10	9	16†	10
State/regional speech contest	7	7	8	6
Major part in a play	17	22*	24†	18
Varsity letter (sports)	34	37†	35*	32
Art competition award	6	7	5	5
Edited school paper	15*	18†	16†	11
Had original writing published	20*	24†	22†	16
National Science Foundation summer program	2	1	1	1
State/regional science contest	4	3	3	2
Scholastic honor society	32†	34†	42†	26
National Merit recognition	10*	14†	12†	7
Highest degree planned				
None, associate, or equivalent	2†	4†	3†	11
Bachelor's degree (B.A., B.S.)	33†	35*	34*	38
Master's degree (M.A., M.S.)	37*	36*	37*	33
Ph.D. or Ed.D.	15†	15†	14*	10
M.D., D.D.S., or D.V.M.	9†	6	8*	4
LL.B. or J.D.	3	2	2	1
B.D.	0.2	0.2	0.4	0.3
Other	1	1	1	2
Probable major field				
Agriculture (including forestry)	0	1	0	2
Biological sciences	5	5	5	4
Business	9†	9†	8†	16
Education	8*	10	8*	11

	Large (%)	Small (%)	Protestant (visible) (%)	National (%)
Engineering	10	3†	4†	11
English	5	6	6	4
Health professions (non-M.D.)	4	3	3	5
History, political science	10*	10*	11*	7
Humanities (other)	6	8*	8*	4
Fine arts	10	11	10	9
Mathematics or statistics	5	6	6	4
Physical sciences	4	4	4	3
Pre-professional	10*	8	11†	6
Psychology, sociology, anthropology	10	13†	12*	8
Other fields (technical)	2	1	1	3
Other fields (nontechnical)	1	2	2	2
Undecided	2	2	2	2
Probable career occupation				
Artist (including performer)	8	10*	7	6
Businessman	10	8*	8*	11
Clergyman	1	1	2	1
College teacher	1	2	2	1
Doctor (M.D. or D.D.S.)	9†	6	8*	4
Educator (secondary)	11*	15	14	15
Elementary teacher	6*	5*	8	9
Engineer	9	2†	3†	9
Farmer or forester	0	1	1	2
Health professional (non-M.D.)	3	3	3	4
Lawyer	6*	4	6*	3
Nurse	2	2	1	2
Research scientist	3	4	4	3
Other choice	18*	23	18*	21
Undecided	13*	15†	14*	10
Number of applications to other colleges				
None	25†	25†	37†	48
One	19	17*	21	21
Two	22†	20†	19*	15
Three	16†	17†	12*	9
Four	9†	11†	6	4
Five or more	10†	10†	5	3
Number of acceptances by other colleges				
None	26†	26†	36†	46
One	30	30	30	29
Two	25†	24†	21†	16
Three	12†	13†	9*	6
Four	4	4	3	2
Five or more	2	2	1	1
Major influences in deciding to attend this college				
Parent or other relative	40†	44	47	46
High school teacher or counselor	22	27*	20*	23
Friends attending this college	12*	15	18	16
Graduate or other college representative	18†	20†	22†	13
Counseling or placement service	8*	5	3	4

	Large (%)	Small (%)	Protestant (visible) (%)	National (%)
Athletic program of the college	7	9*	7	6
Other extracurricular activities	7	9*	6	5
Social life of the college	13†	13†	10	8
Chance to live away from home	26†	23†	21†	15
Low cost	4†	8†	4†	22
Academic reputation of the college	61†	60†	66†	46
Most students are like me	9	14†	15†	9
Religious affiliation	6	6	24†	8
Region of home state				
Middle States	29	31*	24*	28
New England	8	16†	3*	6
North Central	43†	24†	40†	35
Northwest	0*	3	1*	4
Southern	18	19*	27†	16
Western	1†	6*	4†	10
Foreign	1	2	1	1
Father's education				
Grammar school or less	4†	7*	6*	10
Some high school	9†	9†	10†	17
High school graduate	25†	19†	22†	30
Some college	20	18	19	18
College graduate	25†	26†	25†	16
Postgraduate degree	18†	22†	19†	9
Mother's education				
Grammar school or less	3*	4	4	6
Some high school	7	8†	7†	15
High school graduate	40*	31†	34†	43
Some college	24†	23†	24†	19
College graduate	22†	26†	27†	14
Postgraduate degree	5	7*	5	3
Racial background				
Caucasian	92*	90	95†	89
Negro	3*	6	2*	6
American Indian	0.2	0.4	0.2	1
Oriental	1	1	1	1
Other	3	3	2	4
Religious background				
Protestant	48†	60†	84†	54
Roman Catholic	26†	20†	7†	32
Jewish	18†	10†	3	5
Other	5	6	4*	7
None	2	3	1	2
Present religious preference				
Protestant	42†	51	78†	49
Roman Catholic	24†	19†	6†	31
Jewish	16†	9†	2	4
Other	6	8	5*	8
None	11*	13†	8	8

	Large (%)	Small (%)	Protestant (visible) (%)	National (%)
Father's occupation				
Artist (including performer)	2	2	1	1
Businessman	46†	39†	38†	30
Clergyman	1	1	3	1
College teacher	1	2	1	1
Doctor (M.D. or D.D.S.)	6*	6*	5*	2
Educator (secondary)	2	3	3	2
Elementary school teacher	0	0	0	0
Engineer	7	7	8	7
Farmer or forester	2*	3*	5	6
Health profession (non-M.D.)	1	1	1	1
Lawyer	3	4*	2	1
Military career	1	2	2	2
Research scientist	1	1	1	1
Skilled worker	8†	7†	8†	13
Semiskilled worker	4*	5*	4*	8
Unskilled worker	2	2	2	4
Unemployed	0	1	1	1
Other	13†	15*	14*	18
Estimated parental income				
Less than $4,000	2*	5	3	5
$4,000–5,999	5*	6*	6*	9
$6,000–7,999	7†	7†	11*	14
$8,000–9,999	10*	8†	11*	14
$10,000–14,999	22	18*	22	21
$15,000–19,999	11*	10	10	8
$20,000–24,999	6	7*	6	4
$25,000–29,999	5*	4	4	2
$30,000 or more	10†	11†	7*	4
Have no idea	22	26†	19	20
Major sources of financial support during freshman year				
Personal savings or employment	11†	12†	13†	26
Parental or family aid	69†	70†	68†	54
Repayable loan	14	13	16	14
Scholarship, grant, or other gift	26†	20*	24†	7
Concern about financing education				
None	41†	44†	37*	34
Some concern	50†	48†	55	57
Major concern	8	8	8	9
Objectives to be considered essential or very important				
Achieve in a performing art	12	10|	14*	11
Be an authority in my field	71*	69	69	68
Obtain recognition from peers	44	43	42	42
Perform or compose music	8	8	12*	8
Be an expert in finance	12	10	10	11
Be administratively responsible	24	22*	20†	25
Be very well-off financially	47*	40*	35†	44
Help others in difficulty	62	67†	67†	62
Join the Peace Corps or VISTA	18	24†	22*	19

	Large (%)	Small (%)	Protestant (visible) (%)	National (%)
Become an outstanding athlete	15	18*	13	14
Become a community leader	26	28*	30†	24
Contribute to scientific theory	14	12	11	12
Write original works	18*	20†	18*	14
Not be obligated to people	26	25	22*	25
Create works of art	18	21*	17	16
Keep up with political affairs	56†	55†	56†	50
Succeed in my own business	48	44	42*	46
Develop a philosophy of life	86*	88†	88†	83
Students estimate chances are very good that they will				
Get married while in college	6	6	7	8
Marry within year after college	25	24	27*	23
Obtain average grade of A— or higher	3	2	3	3
Change major field	20†	22†	25†	15
Change career choice	21†	26†	28†	16
Fail one or more courses	3	3	3	3
Graduate with honors	4	4	4	4
Be elected to a student office	4	4	3	2
Join social fraternity or sorority	50†	35†	41†	30
Author a published article	8	9*	9*	6
Be elected to an honor society	4	3	4	3
Participate in demonstrations	6	8*	6	5
Drop out temporarily	1	1	1	1
Drop out permanently	1	1	1	1
Transfer to another college	11	14	12	13
I can presently do this well				
Type 40 words per minute	36†	38*	41	42
Sketch recognizable people	9	10	8	9
Speak second language fluently	11	14*	11	11
Break 100 in golf	22†	15	16	14
Water-ski	41†	39*	39*	35
Ski on snow	20*	25†	15	17
Sight-read piano music	25*	25*	28†	21
Read music (singing)	28	31	39†	30
Identify 15 species of birds	14*	16	18	17
Referee a sporting event	40	40	36	38
Recite long passages from memory	15	18*	15	14
Identify architectural styles	17*	18†	15	13
Sail a boat	25†	26†	19*	16
Identify constellations of stars	10	9	8	9
Use a sewing machine	32†	40	40	39
Use Robert's Rules of Order	18	17	19*	16
Mix a dry martini	26†	22	14†	20
Set a table for a formal party	46†	49†	42	41
Name players of professional athletic team	39†	32	32	32
Score a tennis match	43†	42†	40†	34
Identify many music compositions	16*	15*	16*	12
Program a computer	3	2	2	2

	Large (%)	Small (%)	Protestant (visible) (%)	National (%)
Use a slide rule	41†	35	40†	33
Swim a mile without stopping	39†	35†	33*	29
Name the animal phyla	12	12	9	10
Describe difference between stocks and bonds	44*	38*	40	41
Develop and print photographs	9	9	8	8
Bake a cake from scratch	39*	47*	46*	43
Describe the Bill of Rights	54†	50	52*	49
Do at least 15 push-ups	70	62†	63†	68
Agree strongly or somewhat that				
Faculty should make curriculum	85	84	86	85
Married women belong at home	48†	48†	53*	57
Large families should be discouraged	43	46*	47†	42
College sports should be deemphasized	19	27†	22	21
All scientific findings should be published	51†	48*	45	44
Individual cannot change society	36*	34	33	33
Benefit of college is monetary	50†	46†	42†	57
My beliefs are similar to others	67*	64†	68	70
Faculty pay should be based on student evaluation	65*	63	63	62
Student publications should be cleared	40†	44†	47†	53
Women should be drafted	26	24	25	24
Voting age should be 18	64	62*	63*	66
College has right to ban speaker	30†	33†	36*	40
Disadvantaged should be given preferential treatment	36†	40*	39†	44
Colleges are too lax on student protests	40†	40†	46	48
Dating pattern in high school				
One steady girl/boy friend	21	20	23	22
A series of steady dates	23	25*	23	21
A few friends, but no steadies	24	23	23	24
Pretty much played the field	19	18	16	18
Seldom or never dated	13	14	16	16
Percentage of students reporting that during the past year they				
Voted in student election	78†	74	78†	73
Came late to class	57	62†	62†	57
Played a musical instrument	48*	50†	55†	44
Studied in the library	41	44	45*	42
Checked out a library book	54	59*	62†	55
Arranged date for another student	60†	55	52	53
Overslept and missed a class	24*	25*	19	21
Typed a homework assignment	26	28	26	26
Participated in demonstrations	19*	21†	16	16
Were late with homework assignment	74	74	77*	74
Argued with a teacher in class	61†	59†	62†	50
Were guests in a teacher's home	40*	50†	47†	37
Rode on a motorcycle	53*	54	52*	56
Slept or dozed in class	50*	49	49	47

	Large (%)	Small (%)	Protestant (visible) (%)	National (%)
Studied with other students	91	90	91	91
Did extra reading for a class	15	17*	15	14
Took sleeping pills	7	8	7	6
Tutored another student	55†	54†	52†	46
Played chess	47†	40	42	41
Saw a foreign movie	10*	12†	6	7
Took a tranquilizing pill	11	12	12	10
Discussed religion	36*	38†	39†	33
Took vitamins	63	63	63	61
Visited art gallery or museum	76†	81†	75*	71
Took trip of more than 500 miles	71†	76†	71†	66
Got a traffic ticket	23	20	19	21
Missed school because of illness	3	4	4	3
Smoked cigarettes	21*	19	13*	17
Discussed politics	30†	29†	31†	24
Played tennis	60†	61†	60†	55
Drank beer	62†	57*	46†	54
Played bridge	16†	20†	19†	11
Discussed sports	45	42*	45	45
Asked teacher for advice	30*	32†	31†	26
Had vocational counseling	52†	51†	56*	60
Stayed up all night	63	66	61*	64

*Indicates a 3 to 4 percent difference from national norms.

†Indicates a 5 percent or larger difference from national norms.

Appendix B: National Opinion Research Center–Alumni Sample Survey No. 5023

In June 1968, the alumni sample of graduates in June 1961 were polled by the NORC on their attitudes toward higher education. They were asked what their feelings were on their own undergraduate education and its results, what their attitudes were toward higher education in general, and what they wanted in the way of college for their own children. The NORC was acting under a contract from the Carnegie Commission on Higher Education.

In this report the responses of alumni from Protestant (visible) colleges ($N = 986$) and independent liberal arts colleges ($N = 303$) are contrasted with the total sample of the study ($N = 8,035$) and each other. These N's are approximate inasmuch as fluctuations occur when subjects ignored or refused to answer specific items. The following table, then, gives an approximate breakdown of the samples with which we are concerned, except in this table, the data were provided only for the total groups without separate listing of male and female patterns of responses.

Numbers of respondents	Male	Female	Total
Protestant (visible)	417	569	986
Independent liberal arts	171	132	303
All alumni	4,634	3,401	8,035

We looked for responses that vary from the averages of all the schools in the study to give us a picture of the differences and likenesses among alumni seven years after they graduated from their respective schools. The averages of all schools include technical and science universities; private and other universities; and Protestant (invisible), state, Catholic, Negro, and miscellaneous colleges, as well as the Protestant (visible) and independent liberal arts colleges.

The original inspection of the data used a 3 percentage point criterion to indicate importance or meaningfulness. We then decided to use a 5 percentage point difference as a criterion, but we mention items that did not fit this criterion yet seemed to contribute to the trends observed.

Independent Liberal Arts, Small (under 5,000)

Alfred University, Main Campus

Amherst College

Bates College

Bennington College

Berea College

Bowdoin College

Briarcliff College

Carleton College

Chatham College

Claremont Men's College

Colby College

College of Charleston

Connecticut College

Dartmouth College

Fisk University

Gallaudet College

George Williams College

Grinnell College

Hamilton College

Harvey Mudd College

Hollins College

Marietta College

Marlboro College

Middlebury College

Mills College

Morris Harvey College

Mount Holyoke College

Oberlin College

Pitzer College

Pomona College

Reed College

Rockford College

Rollins College, Main Campus

Scripps College

Springfield College

Stephens College

Swarthmore College

Sweet Briar College

Trinity College

Union College

University of Tampa

Vassar College

Washington College

Washington and Lee University

Wellesley College

Wesleyan University

Western New England College

Wheaton College (Massachusetts)

Whitman College

Williams College

Windham College

Independent Liberal Arts, Large (over 5,000)

Adelphi University, Main Campus

Bradley University

Monmouth College (New Jersey)

Pace College, Main Campus

Rider College

Tulane University of Louisiana

University of Hartford

Protestant (Visible)

Allegheny College

Augsburg College

Austin College

Beloit College

Calvin College

Carroll College (Wisconsin)

Concordia College, Moorhead

DePauw University

Dickinson College

Earlham College

Emory and Henry College

Franklin and Marshall College

Gettysburg College

Guilford College

Hamline University

Haverford College

Lake Forest College

Lebanon Valley College

Lindenwood College

MacMurray College

Mary Baldwin College

Occidental College

Randolph Macon Woman's College

University of Redlands

Valparaiso University

Wesleyan College

Wittenberg University

Wofford College

Attitudes about the undergraduate college experience (by percent)

A. Emotional attachment to college (7 years after graduation)

	Strong	Like it	Mixed feelings	Don't like it	Thoroughly dislike
Protestant (visible)	23*	57	16†	4	.3
Independent liberal arts	39†	50†	9	1	.3
All	26	59	11	3	.6

B. I think my college should have

	Protestant (visible)		Independent liberal arts		All	
	Yes	No	Yes	No	Yes	No
Helped me learn to make own decisions	81	19	85*	15	81	19
Trained me for present job	63	37	34†	66†	65	35
Helped me learn to get along with others	73*	27	80†	20†	69	30
Developed my ability to think/express self	100	0	100	0	98	2
Given me broad knowledge of arts/sciences	93*	7	96†	4†	90	10
Prepared me to get ahead in world	68	32	63†	37†	69	30
Expanded my tolerance of people/ideas	96†	4†	95†	5†	89	11
Helped me form valuable, lasting friendships	58*	42	59†	41†	54	46
Helped me form values/goals of life	88†	12†	84*	16*	80	20
Helped me to learn practical, effective ways of helping people	61	39	42†	58†	60	40
Helped me to prepare for marriage, family	44†	56†	22†	73†	39	61

C. My college actually affected me this way

	Protestant (visible)				Independent liberal arts				All			
	Greatly	Somewhat	A little	Not at all	Greatly	Somewhat	A little	Not at all	Greatly	Somewhat	A little	Not at all
Helped me learn to make own decisions	23*	48*	24*	5	22	54	18*	7	20	52	21	7
Trained me for present job	27†	30*	30†	14*	21†	27†	27†	26†	34	34	22	10
Helped me learn to get along with others	33†	48*	15†	4*	22	58†	15†	5	23	45	24	7
Developed my ability to think/express self	47†	41†	10	1	64†	32†	3†	0	41	46	12	1
Gave me broad knowledge of arts/sciences	49†	41	9†	1	57†	36†	7†	1	35	42	20	3
Prepared me to get ahead in world	17	45	31*	7	21*	42†	29	9	18	47	27	7
Expanded my tolerance of people and ideas	45†	36†	15*	4	50†	36†	11†	3*	34	41	19	6
Helped me form valuable, lasting friendships	32†	34	25*	9†	29*	33	30	7†	25	32	29	14
Helped me to learn practical, effective ways to help people	10	32	40	17	4†	31	36	30†	10	32	38	19
Helped me to prepare for marriage, family life	10*	21	37*	32†	4*	18*	30*	48†	7	22	33	37
Helped me form values/goals of life	18	51†	27	4*	30†	41*	18†	10	20	44	28	8

D. Purposes or results of college

	Most important to me personally today			To typical student at my college today		
	Protestant (visible)	Independent liberal arts	All	Protestant (visible)	Independent liberal arts	All
General education	77†	86†	71	55†	78†	47
Having good time	1	3	1	9*	4†	12
Career training	16†	8†	23	32*	16†	36
Developing ability to get along with people	6	3	5	4	2*	6

E. Would like to have

	Protestant (visible)			Independent liberal arts			All		
	More	Same	Less	More	Same	Less	More	Same	Less
Had poetry, art, music	52	45	2	62†	33†	0	53	44	2
Learned history, English, philosophy	49*	48	2	56*	44	0	52	46	2
Learned psychology, sociology	46	50	4	43†	56†	1	48	49	3
Learned science, mathematics	34*	59*	7	30†	58	11*	37	56	7
Had courses related to present job	35	58*	7	32†	52	17†	37	54	8
Read books related to specific courses	37	56*	7	36	60	4	35	60	6
Read books not related to specific courses	64†	33†	3	65†	31†	4	57	39	5
Studied	44	51	4	44	49	7*	46	50	4
Worried about getting good grades	8	57	35	11	58*	30†	10	55	35
Gotten to know faculty	48†	52*	1	53†	46†	1	43	55	2
Participated in extracurricular activities	35*	63*	2	34*	63*	3	38	59	3
Participated in activities of service to others	34	64	2	32*	66*	1	35	62	2
Dated more	30	67	3	35†	62†	3	30	67	3

F. How would you rate now the following aspects of your undergraduate college or university when you attended it?

	Protestant (visible)					Independent liberal arts					All				
	Excellent	*Good*	*Average*	*Poor*	*Does not apply*	*Excellent*	*Good*	*Average*	*Poor*	*Does not apply*	*Excellent*	*Good*	*Average*	*Poor*	*Does not apply*
Caliber of classroom teaching	22*	52	24	2	0	47†	42†	10†	1	0	18	53	26	3	0
Curriculum and course offerings	13†	54†	30*	2	0	35†	50*	13†	1*	0	22	47	27	4	0
Facilities/opportunities—research	8†	26†	51†	14	0	29†	37†	22†	11	0	24	32	30	13	0
Student housing	15	40†	32†	8*	5†	30†	38†	19†	3†	10	16	33	27	11	13
Caliber of students	28†	46	25†	1	0	51†	37†	12†	1	0	20	46	32	2	0
Knowledge/professional standing of faculty	31	48	20	1	0	59†	35†	6†	0	0	29	48	22	2	0
Personal contacts with faculty	18*	42†	30	10†	0	25†	38†	28*	8†	0	15	32	32	21	0

G. Some college graduates were not entirely happy with their undergraduate experience and have made criticisms like the the following. To what extent was each of these true about your college when you attended it?

	Protestant (visible)				Independent liberal arts				All			
	Very true	*Mostly*	*Somewhat*	*Not at all*	*Very true*	*Mostly*	*Somewhat*	*Not at all*	*Very true*	*Mostly*	*Somewhat*	*Not at all*
No sense of community or student participation	3	4†	27†	66†	3	5†	25†	68†	4	10	37	49
Rules were too restrictive	4	13†	40†	43†	2	11*	38†	49†	4	8	32	56
No chance for community service	5	9	31	55	2	8	30	60†	4	10	32	53
No opportunity to understand society or self	3	4	28	65*	1	3*	17†	78†	2	6	29	62
Not intellectually stimulating	2	5	29	64†	0*	1†	19†	79†	3	7	31	59
Pressure for grades too intense	3*	13	49†	35	5	11	44	40*	7	13	44	36

H. What specific courses would you like to have taken more of — or taken at all?

	Protestant (visible)			Independent liberal arts			All		
	1st choice	2nd choice	3rd choice	1st choice	2nd choice	3rd choice	1st choice	2nd choice	3rd choice
Physical science	9	7	11	8	9	11	9	8	9
Biological science	6	8	9	1*	2*	5	4	6	7
Social science	14	17	14*	18*	24†	25†	14	17	18
Humanities	35*	28	26	47†	40†	32†	31	29	26
Engineering	1	1	1	2	1	1	3	3	2
Medicine	0	2	1	1	0	0	1	1	0
Other health	1	1	3	2	0	0	1	1	1
Education	15	11	13	6†	11	7†	15	13	12
Business	10*	11*	12	8†	9†	8†	14	14	14
Law	2	2	0	1	0	2	1	2	2
Other professional	7	10*	9	4	2†	8	6	7	8
Other	1	1	1	1	0	0	1	0	1

I. If you had it to do over again, would you join a fraternity or sorority?

	Protestant (visible)	Independent liberal arts	All
Yes	61†	42*	45
No	39†	58*	55

J. How well do you think your undergraduate college prepared you for graduate or professional school?

	Protestant (visible)	Independent liberal arts	All
Very well	24†	49†	31
Moderately well	63†	41†	56
Not very well	12	5†	12
Not well at all	1	5*	2

K. How well would you say each of the following prepared you for the job you now hold—general college training, major program, graduate or professional training?

	Protestant (visible)			Independent liberal arts			All		
	gct	mp	g/pt	gct	mp	g/pt	gct	mp	g/pt
Very well	27	26*	39	29	24†	50†	27	29	42
Moderately well	58	42†	48	58	48	35†	59	49	44
Not very well	13	22†	7	11	18	9	11	16	9
Not well at all	3	9*	6	2	10*	5	3	6	4
Never went to graduate or professional school		50†			46†			59	

L. Assuming the draft and standing with a college make no difference, do you think the wisest course for a student is to go right on to and through college or to take some time off to gain experience and maturity?

	Protestant (visible)	Independent liberal arts	All
Beneficial—between high school and college	30	33	32
Beneficial—after college entrance	36†	26*	29
Should go right on through	34†	41	39

M. Many people say that actual job requirements change so rapidly it is useless for colleges to train for specific jobs but that the colleges should educate to give general skills and knowledge.

	Protestant (visible)	Independent liberal arts	All
Agree strongly	27	53†	27
Agree somewhat	46*	37†	43
Neutral	7	3*	6
Disagree somewhat	15	6†	16
Disagree strongly	5	1†	7

N. Of how much benefit do you think a college education is to a woman in her capacity as housewife and mother?

	Protestant (visible)	Independent liberal arts	All
Great benefit	59	65†	58
Some benefit	38	33†	38
No benefit	2	0*	3
A handicap	1	2	1

O. Asked to make remarks or comments about their college education—how it helped, fell short of expectations or present needs, etc.,—percent of respondents who made comments.

	Protestant (visible)	Independent liberal arts	All
Made comments	61†	49†	56
Did not respond	39†	51†	44

P. Listed are general aims or goals of a college. (1) How important was it to your faculty and administration? (2) How important do you think it should have been?

	Protestant (visible)					Independent liberal arts					All				
	AT	G	M	L	No	AT	G	M	L	No	AT	G	M	L	No
1. To faculty															
Develop inner character of students	8	44†	39	10†	0*	11	43†	35	9†	3	10	27	37	21	4
Produce capabilities for citizenship	7	34*	44	15*	1*	9*	46†	31†	11†	2	6	31	42	18	4
Make good consumers with good taste	2	15	37	40†	6†	5*	21†	33*	28†	13	2	15	36	34	14
Produce well-rounded students	25†	43†	28†	3†	1	36†	39*	20†	3†	1	14	36	36	12	2
Prepare for useful careers	5†	31†	44†	18†	2	5†	12†	46†	29†	8†	14	40	33	10	2
Develop objectivity regarding self and beliefs	10	39†	41	9†	1*	20†	43†	25†	11†	1*	7	29	39	20	4
Cultivate intellects to maximum	4	28	47*	17*	4	18†	34†	29†	13†	6	6	27	44	20	4
Affect great ideas and minds of history	7	24*	45	20†	3*	8*	26†	47*	13†	6	4	20	44	25	6
Train in scientific method, scholarship, creativity	5	28†	50†	15	2	9	43†	36†	11*	1	9	33	42	14	2

	AT	G	M	L	No	AT	G	M	L	No	AT	G	M	L	No
Disseminate new ideas in all areas	5	16†	43*	29*	7	5	29†	29†	29*	8	6	21	40	25	8
Provide skills for status and leadership	3	26	41*	26*	4	5	28*	41*	15†	11†	5	25	44	22	5
2. Should have been															
Develop inner character of students	15*	51†	29*	5	1	12†	58†	22*	4*	4	18	46	26	7	2
Produce capabilities for citizenship duties	18	49	27	5	0	18	51	24*	5	1	16	50	27	5	1
Make good consumers with good taste	3	25	43†	22	6*	9*	17†	36	19	18†	5	26	38	21	10
Produce well-rounded students	31	52*	16	1	1	38†	45*	12†	4	1	32	48	17	3	1
Prepare students for useful careers	6†	40	33*	20†	1	9†	12†	47†	25†	8†	16	41	30	11	2
Develop objectivity regarding self and beliefs	28*	49	21	2	0	31†	57†	9†	3	0	24	50	22	4	1
Cultivate intellects to maximum	19*	36	29	13*	3	23	41*	25	8	3	22	38	27	10	4
Affect great ideas and minds of history	13	28	40	19	1*	13	24†	42*	14*	6	11	30	38	17	4
Train in scientific method, scholarship, creativity	13†	54*	29*	4	0	20	44†	29*	5	1	20	51	25	4	1
Disseminate new ideas in all areas	16	41	30	11	3	15*	40	25*	15†	5	18	41	29	9	3
Provide skills for status and leadership	7†	29†	39†	21†	5	14	24†	33	16	13†	12	34	33	16	5

AT—absolute top importance; G—great importance; M—medium importance; L—little importance; No—no importance

Q. What kind of school did you go to before college?

	Protestant (visible)		Independent liberal arts		All	
	Grade	High school	Grade	High school	Grade	High school
1. Before college						
Public	93†	88†	74†	65†	81	81
Private denominational (including Catholic)	4†	5†	10*	13	14	14
Private nonsectarian	1	5	6†	16†	1	3
Combination of the above	2	3	9†	5*	3	2

2. *Before getting your bachelor's degree, did you ever attend a two-year junior or community college?*

	Protestant (visible)	Independent liberal arts	All
Yes	4†	1†	12
No	96†	99†	88

3. *Altogether, how many colleges did you attend before you graduated? (Does not include summer attendance.)*

	Protestant (visible)	Independent liberal arts	All
One	83†	88†	72
Two	16†	10†	24
Three	1*	1*	4
Over three	0	0	1

4. *Did you go right on to college after you graduated from high school? If not, how many years were between high school and college?*

	Protestant (visible)	Independent liberal arts	All
5 or more	1*	0†	5
4	1	0	2
3	1	0	2
2	1	0	1
1	5	2	3
0, went right on	92†	97†	87

5. *Did you ever leave college for a period of at least one semester or quarter?*

	Protestant (visible)	Independent liberal arts	All
No	88†	94†	82
Primarily academic reasons	2	4	3
Primarily personal reasons	5	2*	7

	Protestant (visible)	Independent liberal arts	All
Primarily financial reasons	2*	1†	6
Primarily other reasons	3	0	2

R. Estimate as best you can the number of years you have spent full time in graduate or professional degree programs.

	Protestant (visible)	Independent liberal arts	All
None	41	35†	41
Less than one year	12	7*	10
One year	13	14	14
Two years	11	14	13
Three years	8	15†	8
Four years	5	5	5
Five or more years	10	10	8

S. What is the highest degree you now hold; the highest degree you expect to hold?

	Protestant (visible)		Independent liberal arts		All	
	Now hold	Expect to hold	Now hold	Expect to hold	Now hold	Expect to hold
Undergraduate bachelor's	68	35*	54†	32	66	32
Professional (LL.B., M.D., M.S.W., J.D., etc.)	8	8	17†	18†	9	10
Arts and Sciences master's	19	39	23	33†	21	40
Doctorate (Ph.D., Ed. D., Sc.D., etc.)	5	17	5	16	4	17

T. The field in which you took the highest degree you now hold; the field in which you will take the highest degree you expect to hold.

	Highest degree now held			Highest degree expect to hold		
	Protestant (visible)	Liberal arts	All	Protestant (visible)	Liberal arts	All
Physical science	12*	11*	8	12†	9	7
Biological science	3	3	3	2	2	3
Social science	11*	18†	8	9	17†	8
Humanities	17†	28†	12	16†	26†	11
Engineering	2†	2†	9	2†	1†	8
Medicine	1	4	2	1	5*	2
Other health	6	5	4	7*	5	3
Education	29	7†	29	29	8†	30
Business	8†	10*	13	10†	14	15
Law	2	7*	3	2	7*	4
Other professional	8	3*	7	10	6*	9
Other	1	1	1	0	1	1

U. Years in which degrees were received

	Highest degree now held				Highest degree expected		
	Protestant (visible)	Liberal arts	All		Protestant (visible)	Liberal arts	All
1968	2	2	2	1976	1	4	2
1967	6	2*	5	1975	2	1	3
1966	5	4	6	1974	0	0	1
1965	8	10*	7	1973	2	1	2
1964	6	11†	6	1972	3	2	4
1963	4	11†	5	1971	3	3	4
1962	3	6*	3	1970	10	7	9
1961	66	53†	65	1969	4	5	6
1960	0	0	0	1968	7	4	6
				1960–67	67*	73†	64

V. During this academic year (1967–68), have you been enrolled in a program leading to a degree higher than an undergraduate bachelor's degree?

	Protestant (visible)	Independent liberal arts	All
Yes	18	17	17
No	82	83	83

* Indicates a 3 to 4 percent difference from national norms.
† Indicates a 5 percent or greater difference from national norms.

Occupational status

A. How many significantly different jobs have you held since you graduated from college? Count a change in either the type of work or employer, include your present job. How many jobs do you hold now?

Number of jobs held

	Protestant (visible)	Liberal arts	All
Six or more	1	3	2
Five	1	2	3
Four	9	5*	8
Three	19	26†	21
Two	35*	36*	32
One	32	26†	31
None	2	3	2

Number of jobs now

	Protestant (visible)	Liberal arts	All
None	31†	29†	22
One	64†	66†	71
Two or more	5	5	6

B. When did you start working on the job you now hold?

	Protestant (visible)	Liberal arts	All
1968	4	11†	6
1967	21	15†	22
1966	22*	19	18
1965	15*	23†	11
1964	10	8	9
1963	5*	9	8
1962	7	2†	7
1961	15	12†	17
1960 or earlier	1	0	2

C. How many hours a week do you work on the job you now hold?

	Protestant (visible)	Liberal arts	All
51 hours or more	18	22†	16
50 hours	12	20†	11
49-46 hours	6	5	4
45 hours	6*	10	9
44-41 hours	5	3	4
40 hours	24†	27†	33
39-36 hours	5	4	4
35 hours	6	6	6
Under 35	19†	3†	12

D. What is the field that best describes (1) your present job; (2) your anticipated long-run career field?

	Present job			Anticipated career field		
	Protestant (visible)	Liberal arts	All	Protestant (visible)	Liberal arts	All
Physical science	9*	3	5	5	3	4
Biological science	2	3	2	2	2	2
Social science	3	10†	2	3	8†	2
Humanities	7*	6	4	9*	9*	5
Engineering	1†	2†	9	2*	1†	6
Medicine	1	6*	2	1	5*	2
Other health	5	5	3	6	3	4
Education	26	12†	27	26	16†	28
Business	20*	30†	23	17	22*	19
Law	3	6*	3	2	5	3
Other professional	17*	8†	14	13	7†	12
Other	5	9*	5	13	18†	12

E. Census classification of (1) your present job; (2) your anticipated long-run career field.

	Present job			Anticipated long-run career		
	Protestant (visible)	Liberal arts	All	Protestant (visible)	Liberal arts	All
Professional	76†	64†	71	80†	69*	73
Managers	15*	30†	19	18*	26*	22
Clerical	2	1	2	0	4*	1
Sales	2	1	2	0	0	1
Skilled laborers	3	2*	5	0	0	2
Operative	0	0	0	0	0	0
Service workers	1	0	1	1	0	0
Laborers	0	0	0	0	0	0
Farmers	0	0	1	0	0	1
Farm laborers	0	0	0	0	0	0

F. Which of the following best describes (1) the kind of employer you work for now; (2) the kind of employer you expect as your long-range employer?

	Present employer			Expected long-range employer		
	Protestant (visible)	Liberal arts	All	Protestant (visible)	Liberal arts	All
College, university	19†	16*	12	28†	21	22
Research organization, not college	4	0	2	2	2	2
Private company	22†	40†	30	22*	29*	25
Professional office	5*	9	8	6*	14†	9

Self-employed	5	6	4	4	12†	6
Elementary or secondary school system	21*	9†	24	23	12†	23
Federal government	8	11	10	2*	5	5
State government	3	1	3	1	0	1
Other	12*	8	8	12†	5	6

G. Which of these characteristics would be very important to you in picking a job or career?

	Protestant (visible)	*Independent liberal arts*	*All*
Making a lot of money	21†	34*	30
Opportunity to be original and creative	69	74†	67
Opportunity to be helpful to others or useful to society	77†	70	70
Avoiding high-pressure work	27	26	26
Living and working in world of ideas	54	54	53
Freedom from supervision	32†	47†	37
Moderate, steady progress	39*	29†	36
Chance for leadership	54	56	55
Work with people rather than things	67*	66	64
Opportunities for advancement	40†	59†	53
Stable, secure future	35†	34†	44

Whether or not you desire each characteristic, rate your job in terms of the opportunities it gives you for achieving each of the following:

	Protestant (visible)			Independent liberal arts			All		
	Extremely good	Average	Poor	Extremely good	Average	Poor	Extremely good	Average	Poor
Making a lot of money	15*	42*	44†	31†	37†	32*	19	46	35
Opportunity to be original and creative	54	35*	11	52	29†	19†	52	38	10
Opportunity to be helpful to others or useful to society	61	34*	5†	59	32	0	60	30	10
Avoiding high-pressure work	14	57†	29†	14	48*	39†	14	52	34
Living and working with world of ideas	47	39	14	50*	33†	18*	46	40	14
Freedom from supervision	30*	59†	10	45†	42†	13	34	53	12
Moderate, steady progress	44	53*	3*	45*	45†	10*	42	50	7
Chance for leadership	50*	42*	8	49*	40	11	53	38	9
Work with people rather than things	70	24	6	76†	16†	9*	71	23	6
Opportunities for advancement	24†	57†	18*	43†	46†	12*	33	52	15
Stable, secure future	55	39	6	61†	32†	7	54	38	7

H. How much do you want a job to provide the following characteristics?

	Protestant (visible)				Independent liberal arts				All			
	Very much	Some	A little	Not at all	Very much	Some	A little	Not at all	Very much	Some	A little	Not at all
Responsibility	57	41	1	0	70†	30†	0	0	59	40	1	0
Variety in the work	71†	28†	1	0	66	33	1	0	66	33	1	0
Control over what I do	45*	29	22†	4	57†	24†	14*	5	48	30	17	4
Control over others	12*	45*	32†	10	12*	51*	23*	14*	16	48	26	10
Challenge	72*	27†	1	0	83†	15†	2	0	76	22	1	0

My present job provides:

	Protestant (visible)				Independent liberal arts				All			
	As much as I want	Quite a bit	Some	None	As much as I want	Quite a bit	Some	None	As much as I want	Quite a bit	Some	None
Responsibility	53	32	14	0	46†	36*	18†	0	55	33	12	0
Variety in the work	38*	37	22*	3	39*	33†	27†	1	42	39	18	1
Control over what I do	44	33	18	4	39*	33	18	9†	43	35	18	4
Control over others	36	22*	27*	15	32†	25	21*	22†	37	26	24	13
Challenge	48	30	19*	2	45*	33	20*	2	49	32	16	2

I. Are you now teaching or doing research in a college or university with the rank of at least instructor?

	Protestant (visible)	Independent liberal arts	All
No	93	91	93
Teaching only	5	4	4
Research only	0	0	1
Teaching and research both	2	4	2

*Indicates a 3 to 4 percent difference from national norms.
†Indicates a 5 percent or larger difference from national norms.

Personal background and opinions

A. Have you ever served in the armed forces?

	Protestant (visible)	Independent liberal arts	All
No	78†	70	69
Yes, drafted	3	1*	5
Yes, enlisted	19†	29*	26

B. In how many different communities have you lived since graduation? Include present home.

	Protestant (visible)	Independent liberal arts	All
Over 6	6	7	7
5	8	6	7
4	15	13	13
3	29†	25	24
2	28	30	28
1	14†	19	20

C. Do you own or rent your home?

	Protestant (visible)	Independent liberal arts	All
Own outright	9*	16*	12
Buying it now	39*	25†	42
Rent	44†	51†	38
Living with parents	2	4	4
Other	6	4	5

D. Taken altogether, now would you say things are these days? Would you say you are:

	Protestant (visible)	Independent liberal arts	All
Very happy	45*	46*	42
Pretty happy	46†	49	51
Not too happy	8	5	7

E. What is:

	Present religious affiliation			Spouse's present affiliation			Religion in which spouse was reared		
	Protestant (visible)	Liberal arts	All	Protestant (visible)	Liberal arts	All	Protestant (visible)	Liberal arts	All
Roman Catholic	10†	10†	22	13†	10†	22	16†	15†	24
Jewish	1†	17†	7	1†	14†	6	2†	13†	7
Methodist	24†	5†	14	21†	5†	14	23†	10†	16
Baptist	0†	0†	6	1†	1†	7	6†	2†	11
Lutheran	13†	6	7	17†	1†	8	17†	3†	9
Congregationalist	3	2	2	1	1	2	8*	4	4
Presbyterian	14†	15†	9	12	21†	10	12*	16†	9
Episcopalian	7	24†	7	6	26†	7	5	27†	6
Other Protestant	8	3*	6	6	4	6	6	2†	7
Other	3	3	4	2	3	3	3	2	3
None	16	16	15	19†	14	14	2	5	3

F. How frequently do you attend religious services?

	Protestant (visible)	Independent liberal arts	All
Weekly	32†	21†	38
Several times a month	22†	13	15
Once a month	11*	8	8
Two or three times a year	16	29†	17
Once a year	8	12*	8
Never	12	17*	14

G. Which of the following comes closest to your own political leanings?

	Protestant (visible)	Independent liberal arts	All
Conservative Republican	25*	14†	21
Liberal Republican	30†	26†	21
Conservative Democrat	6†	10	12
Liberal Democrat	12†	10†	17
Conservative Independent	10	18†	12
Liberal Independent	14	16	14
"New Left"	1	4*	1
Other	1	1	1

H. How much money do you earn and expect to earn from (1) your own employment; (2) all sources for entire family?

	Now			Expect in 6 years			Expect at age 45		
	Protestant (visible)	Liberal arts	All	Protestant (visible)	Liberal arts	All	Protestant (visible)	Liberal arts	All
$30,000 or over							19*	39†	23
25,000–29,000				5†	23†	11	8*	10	11
20,000–24,000	1	2	2	10	16†	11	14	14	16

	Protestant (visible)	Liberal arts	All	Protestant (visible)	Liberal arts	All	Protestant (visible)	Liberal arts	All
15,000–19,000	3*	12†	7	19†	21*	25	16	14*	18
11,000–14,000	12†	22	20	19	15*	18	7	6	8
10,000	9*	13	12	10	5*	8	10*	2†	7
8,000–9,000	17	13†	18	12*	4*	8	10†	2*	5
5,000–7,000	19*	14	16	8	5	6	5	4	4
1,000–4,000	11†	4	6	6*	0*	3	2	1	1
None	28†	20	19	12*	10	9	8	8	8

All sources for entire family—earned and expected to earn

	Now			Expect in 6 years			Expect at age 45		
	Protestant (visible)	Liberal arts	All	Protestant (visible)	Liberal arts	All	Protestant (visible)	Liberal arts	All
$30,000 or over							39	60†	40
25,000–29,000	6	16†	9	18†	40†	23	17	11†	17
20,000–24,000	21	18	19	19	16*	20	22	15†	20
15,000–19,000	24†	29*	32	36*	22†	32	14	8†	15
11,000–14,000	15	17*	14	18	14	16	4	4	4
10,000	17	10†	15	4	4	5	2	0	2
8,000–9,000	15†	7	9	5	3	3	0	0	1
5,000–7,000	1	2	2	0	1	1	0	1	0
1,000–4,000	0	2	0	0	0	0	0	0	0
None	0	0	0	0	0	0	0	0	0

I. Age of respondent in 1968

	Protestant (visible)	Independent liberal arts	All
40 or over	1	0*	3
35–39	0†	1*	5
34	1	0	2
33	1	1	3
32	2	2	3
31	3	1*	5
30	8†	7†	13
29	69†	73†	52
28	13	14	12
25–27	1	0	1

J. What is your current marital status?

	Protestant (visible)	Independent liberal arts	All
Single, no plans for marriage	14	21†	14
Single, definite plans to be married	1	1	2
Widowed, divorced, separated	2	2	2
Married	84	75†	82

K. Did your spouse attend the same college you did?

	Protestant (visible)	Independent liberal arts	All
Yes, met there	27*	4†	23
Yes, didn't meet there	0†	1†	9
No, different college	60†	87†	46
No, didn't go to college	13†	8†	22

L. Data on children

Number of children you now have

	Protestant (visible)	Independent liberal arts	All
5 or more	0	0	2
4	2	1*	4
3	9†	7†	14
2	35*	48†	39
1	24	26*	23
0	29†	17	18

Ages of

	Oldest son			Oldest daughter		
	Protestant (visible)	Independent liberal arts	All	Protestant (visible)	Independent liberal arts	All
17 or over	2	0	3	0*	1*	4
10-16	2=	1†	6	3*	1†	6
9	1	2	2	0	2	2
8	1	0	2	0*	1	3
7	1*	2	4	2	4	3
6	5*	6*	9	6*	1†	9
5	24†	19*	15	14	10*	14
4	8*	13	12	13	20†	14
3	15	13	13	20†	16*	13
2	25†	18†	13	3†	23†	13
1	12	16	14	28†	15	14
Under 1	5	9†	4	5	5	5

M. Number of children

	You would like to have			Your spouse would like to have		
	Protestant (visible)	Liberal arts	All	Protestant (visible)	Liberal arts	All
7 or more	0	0	1	0	1	0
6	1	2	2	0	4	2
5	3	3	4	4	2	4
4	15*	24†	19	14†	24†	19
3	31	36†	31	34	33	32
2	42†	33*	37	41†	34	36
1	3	0*	3	2	0*	3
0	4	2	3	4	2	3

N. Which of these do you expect to give you more satisfaction in life?

	Protestant (visible)	Independent liberal arts	All
Your career or occupation	19*	25*	22
Family relationships	81*	75*	78

O. How often do you do each of the following?

	Protestant (visible)				Independent liberal arts				All			
	Freq.	Occas.	Rarely	Never	Freq.	Occas.	Rarely	Never	Freq.	Occas.	Rarely	Never
Read nonfiction books	37	46*	16	2	38	40	21*	0	39	42	17	2
Read "serious fiction"	31†	37*	29	3*	32†	38	24*	6	26	40	28	6
Read poetry	7	24*	39*	30	2*	20	46*	32	6	20	42	32
Listen to classical music	41†	34*	21	3*	38†	36	19*	7	32	37	23	7

Go to concerts	10	38†	35	17†	15†	38†	31†	16†	8	33	37	22
Go to plays	14	52†	24†	10	23†	44	26†	7†	13	44	31	12
Go to museums, art galleries	11	45	35	9	18†	40*	34	8	11	44	35	9
Travel abroad	4	19*	18	59	13†	30†	17	40†	6	15	19	60

My college experience was of

	Protestant (visible)			Independent liberal arts			All		
	Great	Moderate influence	No	Great	Moderate influence	No	Great	Moderate influence	No
On:									
Reading nonfiction books	21	53	26	18	65†	17†	20	53	27
Reading "serious fiction"	13	53	34	18*	59†	23†	14	52	34
Reading poetry	15*	32†	53	18†	43†	39†	11	37	52
Listening to classical music	19†	45†	36†	19†	46†	35†	14	38	48
Going to concerts	12	47†	41†	15†	39	46†	10	38	52
Going to plays	15	50†	35†	14*	46*	40†	11	43	45
Going to museums, art galleries	11	48†	41†	20†	51†	29†	10	43	46
Traveling abroad	4	21	74	14†	31†	54†	5	19	76

P. About how many books do you own, including paperbacks?

	Protestant (visible)	Liberal arts	All
Under 50	4†	2†	9
50–74	9	4*	8
75–99	5	5	7
100–149	14	9†	14
150–199	12	8*	11
200–249	12	12	12
250–299	6	11*	7
300–349	6	6	7
350–499	7	19†	7
500–999	12	11	11
1,000 or over	11*	10*	7

Q. When is the last time you visited your college since you graduated?

	Protestant (visible)	Liberal arts	All
1961	1	0	1
1962	6	10†	5
1963	7	5	7
1964	9	5	7

	Protestant (visible)	Liberal arts	All
1965	12*	6	8
1966	16	24†	14
1967	14†	15†	20
1968	14*	10†	18
Never	21	26†	21

R.   Alumni activities

How much money d'd you contribute to your college in the last 12 months?

	Protestant (visible)	Liberal arts	All
$100 or over	2	5*	2
90–99	0	0	0
80–89	0	0	0
70–79	1	0	0
60–69	1	1	0
50–59	5*	5*	2
40–49	0	1	0
30–39	3	3	2
20–29	15†	17†	9
10–19	24†	25†	14
1–10	6	10*	7
None	44†	32†	63

How much do you plan to contribute next year?

	Protestant (visible)	Liberal arts	All
$100 or more	3	5	2
90–99	0	0	0
80–89	0	0	0
70–79	1	1	0
60–69	1	0	0
50–59	7*	7*	4
40–49	1	2	1
30–39	1	2	1
20–29	20†	23†	12
10–19	27†	22†	15
1–10	3*	11*	7
None	36†	26†	58

Is this more or less than you give on the average?

	Protestant (visible)	Liberal arts	All
More	13	25†	11
Same	73†	64†	78
Less	13	10	12

Are you a member of the alumni association of your college?

	Protestant (visible)	Liberal arts	All
Yes	47*	70†	43
No	53*	30†	57

Have you ever tried to interest a young person in attending your college?

	Protestant (visible)	Independent liberal arts	All
Yes, frequently	9*	12	12
Yes, occasionally	31†	41†	36
Yes, rarely	24*	21	21
No	36†	26†	31

S. How do you feel about each of the following proposals for higher education?

	Protestant (visible)				Independent liberal arts				All			
	Agree		Disagree		Agree		Disagree		Agree		Disagree	
	Strongly	Somewhat	Somewhat	Strongly	Strongly	Somewhat	Somewhat	Strongly	Strongly	Somewhat	Somewhat	Strongly
Federal grants to students for college of their choice	16	39	21†	24	19†	34*	28	19	14	37	27	21
Federal loan program covering college costs	42	44	9	4	46†	37†	7	9*	41	45	9	6
No federal aid to operating expenses, only special programs	6†	51†	31	11*	15*	44	27†	14	11	42	33	14
College should go out of existence if dependent on federal aid for survival	4*	18	25*	63†	7	17	20†	56†	8	19	28	45
If given state aid, college should be subject to state supervision	6†	34†	28†	32†	7†	36*	15†	42†	16	40	20	24
State legislature should raise taxes to support higher education	15	40	34*	11*	12*	44	33*	12	15	42	30	14
States should let other programs suffer to support higher education	4	22*	52†	22	7	21†	55†	18*	6	26	46	22
College should charge real costs; government should loan to students to meet them	8*	32†	40†	20*	8*	37	40†	14*	11	37	35	17
College expenses should be tax-deductible for parents	69*	23*	7	1	69*	19†	10*	3	65	27	6	3

T. Which of the following should receive federal aid for operating expenses? State support?

Federal

	Protestant (visible)	Liberal arts	All
Public colleges only	19*	20	22
Public and private/no religious affiliation	9†	21†	16
All colleges	55†	48*	45
No colleges	16	11†	17

State

	Protestant (visible)	Liberal arts	All
Private colleges/no religious affiliation	12†	22*	19
All private	56†	43	42
No private	32†	35*	39

U. Who should receive financial aid to go to college?

	Protestant (visible)				Liberal arts				All			
	Agree		Disagree		Agree		Disagree		Agree		Disagree	
	Strongly	Somewhat	Somewhat	Strongly	Strongly	Somewhat	Somewhat	Strongly	Strongly	Somewhat	Somewhat	Strongly
All high school graduates have a right to 2 years of education after high school	15*	21†	28	36†	14*	32†	25	30	18	26	26	30
Government aid to all intelligent students regardless of financial need	3	15*	32	49	4	12	28†	56†	5	12	34	49
Government aid to only those who really need it	39	38	16	6	40	43*	10†	7	38	39	16	7
Federal government should make effort to get minority-group members to college	25†	37	19†	19	21	44†	25	10†	19	37	24	20

V. What proportion of high school students do you think intelligent enough to deserve support for their college education?

	Protestant (visible)	Liberal arts	All
100%	0	3	1
90–99%	2	3	1
80–89%	1	3	3
70–79%	6	8	8
60–69%	9	7	8
50–59%	18	16	16
40–49%	7	6	7
30–39%	10	9	11
20–29%	17	12†	17
10–19%	11	9	10
0–9%	2	4	4
No response	17	21	14

W. The role of students in the operation of our colleges and universities has become an issue on many campuses. How do you feel about each of the following?

	Protestant (visible)				Liberal arts				All			
	Agree		Disagree		Agree		Disagree		Agree		Disagree	
	Strongly	Somewhat	Somewhat	Strongly	Strongly	Somewhat	Somewhat	Strongly	Strongly	Somewhat	Somewhat	Strongly
College should assume responsibility for student behavior, just as parents do	7*	33*	37†	22	6*	38	34	22	10	36	32	23
Students are capable of regulating selves; college should stay out	5	31*	44	20	9	35†	40†	16*	7	27	46	20
Rules about student behavior should be made by students	16†	49*	32	4†	14*	45	34*	8†	11	45	30	13
College shouldn't try to stop students taking part in politics	42†	46	10*	2	41†	44*	13	3	36	47	14	3
Students have right to protest recruiters if felt to be immoral	24*	32	26*	18	28	27†	20	25	21	32	22	25
Students should make the rules governing off-campus political activity	24*	50†	19†	7*	25*	35†	27*	13*	21	45	24	10
College has responsibility to see that students don't break the law	24*	36	36†	14*	25*	32	23†	20*	21	34	28	17
Students have the right to participate in decisions on												
Faculty tenure	1	15	31*	53	2	16	33†	48†	3	15	28	54
Organization of curriculum	8	60†	18†	14†	16†	54*	17†	12†	10	51	21	19
What is taught in specific courses	4	41*	32	23†	7	29†	40†	24*	5	37	31	28
Admissions standards	2	19	34	44*	4	13*	43†	41†	3	17	34	47
Tuition and fees	1	13†	40†	46	3	9†	41†	46	3	17	34	47
Rules about student behavior should be enforced by the students	23*	55	18	4*	26†	53	14†	7	20	53	19	8

X. Some feel today's students are very different from what they were when you were in college. Today's students are:

	Protestant (visible)					Independent liberal arts					All				
	MM	SM	AS	SL	ML	MM	SM	AS	SL	ML	MM	SM	AS	SL	ML
Radical	24	57†	20*	0	0	23	47*	30†	0	0	24	51	24	0	0
Politically minded	38	48	14	0	0	38	49	13	0	0	36	48	15	0	0
Serious	7	21	63	7*	1	5	25†	62	7*	1	6	20	61	10	2
Moral	1	3	51	34	10	2	3	53*	32*	9	1	3	50	35	10

MM – much more; SM – somewhat more; AS – about the same; SL – somewhat less; ML – much less.

Y-1. **Have you ever done any of the following?**

	Protestant (visible)		Liberal arts		All	
	Yes	No	Yes	No	Yes	No
Experimented with drugs	4	96	5	95	4	96
Participated in antiwar protest	7	93	8*	92*	5	95
Participated in civil rights protest	12*	88*	13*	87*	9	91
Worked full-time for a service organization (AFSC, Vista, etc.)	3	97	3	97	2	98
Volunteered to help others (tutoring, in mental hospital, etc.)	55†	45†	55†	45†	43	57

Y-2. **Do you think you would approve or disapprove if one of your college-age children did any of the following?**

	Protestant (visible)			Liberal arts			All		
	Approve	Be neutral	Disapprove	Approve	Be neutral	Disapprove	Approve	Be neutral	Disapprove
Experimented with drugs	0	6	94	2	10†	88†	1	5	94
Participated in antiwar protest	22	42*	36	24	39	38	24	39	38
Participated in civil rights protest	40†	40	20†	39†	43	18†	30	41	29
Worked full time for a service organization (AFSC, etc.)	78†	20*	2	80†	17†	3	73	24	3
Volunteered to help others (tutoring, etc.)	95*	5*	0	93	7	1	91	8	0

Z. Do you think:

	Protestant (visible)				Independent liberal arts				All			
	Agree		Disagree		Agree		Disagree		Agree		Disagree	
	Strongly	Somewhat	Somewhat	Strongly	Strongly	Somewhat	Somewhat	Strongly	Strongly	Somewhat	Somewhat	Strongly
Protests of college students are a healthy sign for America	18*	41*	29	12†	22†	39	29	11†	14	37	31	18
Scientific research is making the world change too fast	1*	22	40	36*	5	21	45*	29*	4	22	41	33
U.S. would be better off with less campus protests and demonstrations	12*	30†	37†	20*	12*	24†	43†	20*	16	35	31	17
Experts have so much power in our society, we don't have much say	7	37†	35†	20	4*	26†	54†	15*	7	32	42	19
Negro protests in cities will be healthy for U.S. in long run	21	40*	26	12†	18	40*	30†	12†	19	37	25	19
Main cause of Negro riots in the cities is white racism	17*	26*	33	24†	16*	20*	33	31	13	23	32	32
Negro militancy is needlessly dividing U.S. in conflicting camps	28	39	26	7	23*	39	29*	9	26	41	25	8
Graduating from a good, not any, college is necessary for a good job	2	24	47*	27	8*	17†	45	31	4	23	44	29
College students should get draft deferments	28	46*	20	6*	38†	28†	19	15†	27	42	21	10
Graduate students should get draft deferments	30*	37	24	9†	30*	29†	18†	22†	27	36	23	14
College students should lose draft deferments for antidraft demonstrations	14†	17	28†	40†	20*	11†	23	46†	24	19	23	34

* Indicates a 3 to 4 percent difference from national norms.

† Indicates a 5 percent or larger difference from national norms.

College for your children

A. Which of your children do you expect to go to college?

	Boys			Girls		
	Protestant (visible)	*Liberal arts*	*All*	*Protestant (visible)*	*Liberal arts*	*All*
All	94	98†	93	88	94†	86
Some	6	2*	6	12	6†	13
None	0	0	0	0	0	1

B. How much do you think it will cost to cover the college expenses of one of your children for a year?

	Protestant (visible)	*Liberal arts*	*All*
$9,990+	2	2	1
9,000–9,980	0	0	0
7,600–8,999	1	2	1
6,600–7,599	1	1	1
5,600–6,599	2	9†	2
4,600–5,599	16†	21†	11
3,600–4,599	18*	21†	14
2,600–3,599	37†	31*	28
1,600–2,599	18†	9†	31
1,000–1,599	4†	1†	10
500–999	1	0	1
Under $500	0	1	1

C. What financial arrangements have you made so far for your children's college education? (Totals = + 100% due to multiple responses.)

	Protestant (visible)	Independent liberal arts	All
Nothing	42	43*	40
Started savings account for college	29*	27	26
Bought insurance to help cover costs	20	15†	22
Made investments	25†	38†	31
Set up a trust fund	3	3	4

D. Roughly how large a school would you like your oldest son and oldest daughter to attend?

	Son			Daughter		
	Protestant (visible)	Liberal arts	All	Protestant (visible)	Liberal arts	All
Under 1,000	4	22†	6	10	31†	11
1,000–1,999	28†	28†	19	37†	30†	25
2,000–4,999	48†	39†	34	41†	29*	32
5,000–9,999	14†	9†	23	10†	7†	19
Over 10,000	5†	2†	16	2†	2†	13

E. What percentage will each of the following contribute to your children's college education?

	Protestant (visible)					Independent liberal arts					All				
	Parents	Child's job	Loan	Scholarships	Other	Parents	Child's job	Loan	Scholarships	Other	Parents	Child's job	Loan	Scholarships	Other
100%	10	0	0	1	1	21†	0	0	0	0	10	0	0	0	0
96-99	1	0	0	0	0	0	0	0	0	0	1	0	0	0	0
86-95	10	0	0	0	0	11	0	0	0	0	10	0	0	0	0
76-85	12	0	0	0	1	12	0	0	0	0	12	0	0	0	0

	Protestant (visible)					Independent liberal arts					All				
	Absolute top	Great	Medium	Little	No	Absolute top	Great	Medium	Little	No	Absolute top	Great	Medium	Little	No
66-75	19	0	0	21	0	0	0	0	0	19	0	0	0	0	0
56-65	8	0	0	4*	0	0	0	0	0	8	0	0	0	0	0
46-55	24	0*	5	17†	1	2	1	4	1	24	3	1	4	1	1
36-45	4	1	2	1*	0	1	3	2	1	4	2	1	2	0	0
26-35	3	6	5	5	2	2*	2	1*	0	4	6	2	4	2	0
16-25	7	28	23*	5	2	24*	14	16*	2	6	28	13	20	13	1
6-15	1	31	20	1	3	30	11*	13†	3	1	29	14	20	14	1
0-5	2	11	5	0	1	8	1	4	0	1	9	2	5	5	0
None	22	69*	40†	92*	93	34†	67	60†	93	22	22	66	45	95	1

F. How important do you think each of the following is in choosing a college for your oldest child of the same sex as you?

	Protestant (visible)					Independent liberal arts					All				
	Absolute top	Great	Medium	Little	No	Absolute top	Great	Medium	Little	No	Absolute top	Great	Medium	Little	No
Low cost	14	29†	52	5†	0	28†	27*	40†	4†	0	13	23	52	11	1
High academic standing	0	3	15	60	22	2	0	11†	53†	33†	1	1	16	58	24
Excellent training for graduate or professional school	1	7	36†	50*	6†	4*	7	40†	38†	12	1	7	31	47	14

G. How desirable do you think each of the following characteristics would be for your oldest child of the same sex as you?

	Protestant (visible)					Independent liberal arts					All				
	Absolutely	Great	Medium	Little	No	Absolutely	Great	Medium	Little	No	Absolutely	Great	Medium	Little	No
College close to home	4*	26†	43*	19*	8*	3*	18†	42*	28†	8*	7	34	39	16	4
Can join fraternity, sorority	12*	26	42*	14	6	2†	16†	44	20†	17†	8	27	45	14	7
Good general education	84†	14†	1	2	0	83†	17*	0	0	0	77	21	1	0	0
Good career training	34†	51†	14*	1	0	29†	43*	22†	6†	1	48	40	10	1	0
Gives a lot of personal freedom	17†	40	23	18	2	20†	52†	19†	8†	1	12	41	24	20	3
Gives good religious education	9	29†	48	10	4†	1†	19†	48	18†	14†	10	24	48	10	9
Students of same social background	8*	24†	38*	22†	8	2*	24†	39	23†	11†	5	30	41	17	6
Faculty and administration concerned with students' personality development	41†	48	10*	1	0	30†	51*	13	4	1	36	48	13	2	1
Extensive athletic program	6	29	54	10	1	6	30	49†	13†	2	6	30	54	8	2
Same college I graduated from	1	15	71	10*	2	7†	21†	62†	6	4	2	16	71	6	4

* Indicates a 3 to 4 percent difference from national norms.

† Indicates a 5 percent or larger difference from national norms.

Appendix C:
Survey of Presidents' Opinions on Financing of Colleges

While he was with the Carnegie Commission staff, Mr. Ronald Wolk surveyed the opinions of presidents, including those of 58 institutions of the type treated in this brochure, about the problems of financing their colleges. Seventy-four percent were operating with a balanced budget and twenty-one percent at a deficit (five percent gave no tabulable answer). A high proportion of those "in the black" expressed fears that tuition was at a breaking point and that program improvements would be postponed or eliminated. Twelve of thirty-four commenting on the point had deferred some "necessary" programs, while five others had deferred "desirable" programs. Three had postponed expansion. Twenty-two of the fifty-eight responding expected to be able to keep revenues up with expenditures, at least for the near future. About twenty-five percent of the fifty-eight expressed great uncertainty, some few sounding a note of desperation.

Sixty-seven percent of those responding thought that better management can help somewhat, but not much, toward meeting the financial problems of these colleges. Only twelve percent thought considerable improvement in efficiency possible, and only five percent thought that such improvement should or could be sought in curriculum management. Here again a few (seven percent) sounded rather despondent about gaining significant advantages through better management. The most frequent suggestions being considered for their own use in gaining efficiency were: year-round use of plant, evening classes, six-day weeks, better classroom utilization, managing enrollment to get efficient class size, judicious use of part-time faculty, accepting conferences and seminars by outside groups to get better use of facilities and to draw upon their services, sharing of curriculum with other colleges, increased teaching loads, reduction of small classes and firmer control over course proliferation, fuller use of computers, and further development of the use of contracted services in areas such as maintenance, food services, and the like.

The respondents to Mr. Wolk's questions were presidents of the following fifty colleges, as well as eight who wished to remain anonymous.

Alliance College	Morris Harvey College*
Azusa Pacific College*	Nasson College*
Bates College*	New College, Florida*
Berea College	Norwich College*
Berry College*	Oberlin College*
Bowdoin College*	Pitzer College
Brenau College*	Reed College*
Carleton College*	Rider College
Chatham College*	Rollins College*
Claremont Graduate School	St. Johns College*
Colby College	Smith College
The Colorado College*	Stephens College*
Connecticut College*	Union College, Schenectady*
Fairleigh Dickinson University*	University of Baltimore*
Gallaudet College*	University of Bridgeport*
George Williams College	University of Tampa*
Grinnell College*	Upper Iowa College*
Hamilton College	Wabash College*
Hofstra University*	Washington College, Maryland*
Hollins College*	Wellesley College*
Judson College	Wells College*
Lake Erie College*	Western College for Women*
Little Rock University*	Wheaton College, Massachusetts*
Marietta College*	Wilkes College*
Monmouth College	Windham College

*Also among the 99 colleges supplying documents for Mr. Keeton's study.

Appendix D:
Private Liberal Arts Colleges in the United States, 1968-69

This list of 700 institutions was tabulated by the Carnegie Commission from data provided by the National Center for Educational Statistics. It consists of three categories of colleges: private independent nonprofit colleges, colleges of Roman Catholic affiliation, and colleges of other religious (generally Protestant) affiliation. A college which has a distinctive religious commitment or character may, nevertheless, be a private independent college in its legal control, and this listing pertains to legal control only.

	Independent	Roman Catholic	Other religious affiliation
Alabama			
Athens College			x
Birmingham Southern College			x
Daniel Payne College			x
Huntingdon College			x
Judson College			x
Miles College			x
Mobile College			x
Oakwood College			x
St. Bernard College		x	
Selma University			x
Spring Hill College		x	
Stillman College			x
Talladega College	x		
Alaska			
Alaska Methodist University			x

	Independent	Roman Catholic	Other religious affiliation
Arizona			
Grand Canyon College			x
Prescott College	x		
Arkansas			
Arkansas Baptist College			x
Arkansas College			x
College of the Ozarks			x
Harding College—Main Campus			x
Hendrix College			x
John Brown University	x		
Philander Smith College			x
California			
Azusa Pacific College	x		
Biola College	x		
California Baptist College			x
California Lutheran College			x
Chapman College	x		
Claremont Men's College	x		
College of Holy Names		x	
College of Notre Dame		x	
Dominican College of San Rafael		x	
Harvey Mudd College	x		
Immaculate Heart College		x	
John F. Kennedy University	x		
LaVerne College			x
Marymount College		x	
Mills College	x		
Mt. St. Mary's College		x	
Occidental College	x		
Pacific College			x
Pacific Oaks College	x		
Pacific Union College			x
Pasadena College			x
Pepperdine College	x		
Pitzer College	x		
Pomona College	x		

	Independent	Roman Catholic	Other religious affiliation
Russell College		x	
St. John's College		x	
St. Mary's College		x	
St. Patrick's College		x	
San Francisco College for Women		x	
San Luis Rey College		x	
Scripps College	x		
Southern California College			x
Tahoe Paradise College	x		
University of Redlands			x
University of San Diego, Men		x	
University of San Diego, Women		x	
Westmont College	x		
Whittier College	x		
Colorado			
Colorado Alpine College	x		
Colorado College	x		
Colorado Western College	x		
Loretto Heights College		x	
Regis College		x	
Temple Buell College	x		
Connecticut			
Albertus Magnus College		x	
Annhurst College		x	
College of Notre Dame of Wilton		x	
Connecticut College	x		
Diocesan Sisters College		x	
Sacred Heart University	x		
St. Joseph College		x	
Trinity College	x		
Wesleyan University	x		
District of Columbia			
Dunbarton College of Holy Cross		x	
Gallaudet College	x		
St. Paul's College		x	
Trinity College		x	

	Independent	Roman Catholic	Other religious affiliation
Florida			
Barry College		x	
Bethune College	x		
Biscayne College		x	
Drake College	x		
Florida Memorial College	x		
Florida Presbyterian College			x
Florida Southern College			x
New College	x		
Rollins College — Main Campus	x		
St. Leo College		x	
Georgia			
Agnes Scott College			x
Atlanta University	x		
Berry College	x		
Brenau College	x		
Clark College	x		
Covenant College			x
La Grange College			x
Morehouse College	x		
Morris Brown College			x
Oglethorpe College	x		
Paine College			x
Piedmont College	x		
Shorter College			x
Spelman College	x		
Tift College			x
Wesleyan College			x
Hawaii			
Chaminade College of Honolulu		x	
Church College of Hawaii			x
Hawaii Loa College			x
Idaho			
College of Idaho			x
Northwest Nazarene College			x

	Independent	Roman Catholic	Other religious affiliation
Illinois			
Augustana College			x
Aurora College			x
Barat College of Sacred Heart		x	
Blackburn College	x		
College of St. Francis		x	
Columbia College	x		
Delourdes College		x	
Elmhurst College			x
Eureka College			x
George Williams College	x		
Greenville College			x
Illinois College	x		
Knox College	x		
Lake Forest College			x
Lewis College	x		
MacMurray College			x
McKendree College			x
Millikin University			x
Monmouth College			x
Mundelein College	x		
North Central College			x
North Park College and Theological Seminary			x
Olivet Nazarene College			x
Principia College	x		
Quincy College		x	
Rockford College	x		
Rosary College	x		
St. Dominic College		x	
St. Procopius College		x	
St. Xavier College		x	
Shimer College	x		
Tolentine College		x	
Trinity College			x
Wheaton College	x		

	Independent	Roman Catholic	Other religious affiliation
Indiana			
Anderson College			x
Bethel College			x
Concordia College			x
DePauw University			x
Earlham College—Main Campus			x
Earlham College—Indiana Center			x
Franklin College of Indiana	x		
Goshen College and Biblical School			x
Grace Theological Seminary and College			x
Hanover College			x
Huntington College			x
Manchester College			x
Marian College—Indianapolis		x	
Marion College of Marion			x
Oakland City College			x
St. Benedict College		x	
St. Francis College		x	
St. Joseph College—Main Campus		x	
St. Joseph College—Calumet		x	
St. Mary of the Woods		x	
St. Mary's College		x	
St. Meinrad Seminary		x	
Taylor University	x		
Tri-State College	x		
Wabash College	x		
Iowa			
Briar Cliff College		x	
Buena Vista College			x
Central University of Iowa			x
Clarke College		x	
Coe College	x		
Cornell College	x		
Divine Word College		x	
Dordt College			x

	Independent	Roman Catholic	Other religious affiliation
Graceland College			x
Grinnell College	x		
Iowa Wesleyan College			x
Loras College		x	
Luther College			x
Marycrest College		x	
Midwestern College	x		
Morningside College			x
Mount Mercy College		x	
Northwestern College			x
Parsons College	x		
St. Ambrose College		x	
Simpson College			x
University of Dubuque			x
Upper Iowa University	x		
Wartburg College			x
Westmar College			x
William Penn College			x
Kansas			
Baker University			x
Bethany College			x
Bethel College			x
College of Emporia			x
Friends University			x
Kansas Wesleyan University			x
Marymount College		x	
McPherson College			x
Mid-American Nazarene College			x
Mt. St. Scholastica College		x	
Ottowa University			x
Sacred Heart College		x	
St. Benedict's College		x	
St. Mary of the Plains College		x	
St. Mary's College		x	
Southwestern College			x
Sterling College			x

	Independent	Roman Catholic	Other religious affiliation
Tabor College			x
Kentucky			
Asbury College	x		
Bellarmine-Ursuline College		x	
Berea College	x		
Brescia College		x	
Campbellsville College			x
Catherine Spalding College		x	
Centre College of Kentucky	x		
Cumberland College			x
Georgetown College			x
Kentucky Southern College	x		
Kentucky Wesleyan College			x
Nazareth College		x	
Pikeville College			x
Thomas More College		x	
Transylvania College	x		
Union College			x
Louisiana			
Centenary College			x
Dillard University			x
Our Lady Holy Cross College		x	
St. Mary's Dominican College		x	
Xavier University		x	
Maine			
Bates College	x		
Bowdoin College	x		
Colby College	x		
Nasson College	x		
Ricker College	x		
St. Francis College		x	
St. Joseph's College		x	
Maryland			
College of Notre Dame		x	
Columbia Union			x
Eastern College	x		

	Independent	Roman Catholic	Other religious affiliation
Goucher College	x		
Hood College	x		
Loyola College		x	
Mt. St. Agnes College		x	
Mt. St. Mary's College		x	
St. John's College—Main Campus	x		
St. Joseph College		x	
St. Mary's Seminary and University		x	
Washington College	x		
Western Maryland College			x
Massachusetts			
Amherst College	x		
Anna Maria College for Women		x	
Assumption College		x	
Atlantic Union College			x
Cardinal Cushing College		x	
College of Our Lady of the Elms		x	
College of the Holy Cross		x	
College of the Sacred Hearts		x	
Curry College	x		
Eastern Nazarene College			x
Emerson College	x		
Emmanuel College		x	
Gordon College	x		
Hellenic College			x
Lesley College	x		
Mount Holyoke College	x		
Newton College of the Sacred Heart		x	
Regis College for Women	x		
St. Hyacinth College and Seminary		x	
Simmons College	x		
Smith College	x		
Springfield College	x		
Stonehill College		x	
Wellesley College	x		
Wheaton College	x		

	Independent	Roman Catholic	Other religious affiliation
Wheelock College	x		
Williams College	x		
Michigan			
Adrian College			x
Albion College			x
Alma College	x		
Aquinas College		x	
Calvin College			x
Duns Scotus College		x	
Hillsdale College	x		
Hope College	x		
Kalamazoo College			x
Mackinac College	x		
Madonna College		x	
Marygrove College		x	
Mercy College of Detroit		x	
Michigan Lutheran College			x
Nazareth College	x		
Olivet College	x		
Owosso College			x
St. Mary's College		x	
Siena Heights College		x	
Society of Arts and Crafts	x		
Spring Arbor College			x
Minnesota			
Augsburg College			x
Bethel College and Seminary			x
Carleton College	x		
College of St. Benedict		x	
College of St. Catherine		x	
College of St. Scholastica		x	
College of St. Theresa		x	
College of St. Thomas		x	
Concordia College—Moorehead			x
Concordia College of St. Paul			x
Dr. Martin Luther College			x

	Independent	Roman Catholic	Other religious affiliation
Gustavus Adolphus College			x
Hamline University			x
Lea College	x		
Macalester College			x
St. John's University		x	
St. Mary's College		x	
St. Olaf College			x
Mississippi			
Belhaven College			x
Blue Mountain College			x
Millsaps College			x
Mississippi College			x
Mississippi Industrial College			x
Rust College			x
Tougaloo College	x		
Whitworth College	x		
William Carey College			x
Missouri			
Avila College		x	
Cardinal Glennon College		x	
Central Methodist College			x
Culver Stockton College			x
Drury College	x		
Evangel College			x
Fontbonne College		x	
Lindenwood College			x
Marillac College		x	
Maryville College of Sacred Heart		x	
Missouri Valley College			x
Notre Dame College		x	
Park College			x
School of the Ozarks			x
Southwest Baptist College			x
Stephens College	x		
Tarkio College			x
Webster College	x		

	Independent	Roman Catholic	Other religious affiliation
Westminster College			x
William Jewell College			x
William Woods College	x		
Montana			
Carroll College		x	
Rocky Mountain College			x
Nebraska			
College of St. Mary		x	
Dana College			x
Doane College			x
Hastings College			x
Hiram Scott College	x		
John F. Kennedy College	x		
John J. Pershing College	x		
Midland Lutheran College			x
Nebraska Wesleyan University	x		
Union College			x
New Hampshire			
Belknap College, Inc.	x		
Cannan College	x		
Franconia College	x		
Franklin Pierce College	x		
Mt. St. Mary College	x		
Nathaniel Hawthorne College	x		
New England College	x		
Notre Dame College		x	
Rivier College		x	
St. Anselm's College		x	
New Jersey			
Alma White College			x
Bloomfield College			x
Caldwell College for Women		x	
College of St. Elizabeth	x		
Don Bosco College		x	
Felician College		x	

	Independent	Roman Catholic	Other religious affiliation
Georgian Court College		x	
St. Peter's College		x	
Shelton College	x		
Upsala College			x
New Mexico			
The College of Artesia	x		
College of Santa Fe		x	
College of the Southwest	x		
St. John's College—Santa Fe	x		
New York			
Bard College	x		
Briarcliff College	x		
Catholic College of the Immaculate Conception		x	
Colgate University	x		
College of Mt. St. Vincent	x		
College of New Rochelle		x	
College of St. Rose		x	
Columbia University—Barnard College	x		
Dominican College of Blauvelt	x		
Dowling College	x		
D'Youville College		x	
Eisenhower College	x		
Finch College	x		
Friends World College	x		
Good Counsel College		x	
Hamilton College	x		
Hartwick College			x
Hobart and William Smith College	x		
Houghton College			x
Iona College		x	
Keuka College	x		
Kings College	x		
Kirkland College	x		
Ladycliff College		x	

	Independent	Roman Catholic	Other religious affiliation
Le Moyne College		x	
Long Island University—South-ampton	x		
Manhattan College		x	
Manhattanville College of Sacred Heart	x		
Marist College	x		
Marymount College		x	
Marymount Manhattan College		x	
Mary Rogers College		x	
Mercy College	x		
Mt. St. Mary College		x	
Nazareth College—Rochester		x	
Notre Dame College—Staten Island		x	
Nyack Missionary College			x
Roberts Wesleyan College			x
Rosary Hill College	x		
St. Francis College		x	
St. John Fischer College, Inc.	x		
St. Joseph College for Women	x		
St. Lawrence College	x		
St. Thomas Aquinas College		x	
Sarah Lawrence College	x		
Siena College		x	
Skidmore College—Main Campus	x		
Vassar College	x		
Wadhams Hall Seminary-College		x	
Wagner College			x
Wells College	x		
North Carolina			
Barber Scotia College			x
Belmont Abbey College		x	
Bennett College			x
Campbell College			x
Catawba College			x
Davidson College			x

	Independent	Roman Catholic	Other religious affiliation
Elon College			x
Greensboro College			x
Guilford College			x
High Point College			x
Johnson College Smith University			x
Lenoir-Rhyne College			x
Livingstone College			x
Mars Hill College			x
Meredith College			x
Methodist College			x
North Carolina Wesleyan College			x
Pfeiffer College, Inc.			x
Queens College			x
Sacred Heart College		x	
St. Andrew's Presbyterian College			x
St. Augustine's College			x
Salem College			x
Shaw University	x		
Warren Wilson College			x
North Dakota			
Jamestown College			x
Mary College		x	
Ohio			
Antioch College — Main Campus	x		
Baldwin-Wallace College			x
Bluffton College			x
Cedarville College			x
College of Mt. St. Joseph on the Ohio		x	
College of Steubenville		x	
College of Wooster			x
Defiance College	x		
Denison University	x		
Findlay College			x
Heidelberg College			x
Hiram College	x		

	Independent	Roman Catholic	Other religious affiliation
Kenyon College			x
Lake Erie College	x		
Malone College			x
Marietta College	x		
Mary Manse College		x	
Mt. Union College			x
Muskingum College			x
Notre Dame College		x	
Oberlin College	x		
Ohio Dominican College		x	
Ohio Northern University—Main Campus			x
Ohio Northern University—Riverside			x
Ohio Wesleyan University			x
Otterbein College			x
Our Lady of Cincinnati College		x	
Rio Grande College	x		
St. John College of Cleveland		x	
Tiffin University	x		
Urbana College			x
Ursuline College		x	
Walsh College		x	
Western College for Women	x		
Wilberforce University			x
Wilmington College			x
Wittenberg University			x
Oklahoma			
Bethany Nazarene College			x
Oklahoma Christian College	x		
Oral Roberts University	x		
Oregon			
Cascade College	x		
George Fox College			x
Linfield College			x
Maryhurst College	x		

	Independent	Roman Catholic	Other religious affiliation
Mt. Angel College		x	
Northwest Christian College			x
Pacific University	x		
Reed College	x		
Warner Pacific College			x
Willamette University	x		
Pennsylvania			
Albright College			x
Allegheny College	x		
Allentown-St. Francis de Sales College		x	
Alliance College	x		
Alvernia College		x	
Beaver College			x
Bryn Mawr College	x		
Cabrini College		x	
Cedar Crest College			x
Chatham College	x		
Chestnut Hill College		x	
College Misercordia		x	
Dickinson College	x		
Eastern Baptist College			x
Elizabethtown College			x
Franklin and Marshall College	x		
Gettysburg College	x		
Grove City College	x		
Gwynedd Mercy College	x		
Haverford College	x		
Holy Family College		x	
Immaculata College		x	
Juniatta College	x		
Kings College	x		
LaFayette College			x
LaRoche College		x	
Lebanon Valley College			x
Lincoln University	x		

	Independent	Roman Catholic	Other religious affiliation
Lycoming College			x
Mercyhurst College		x	
Messiah College			x
Moravian College—Main Campus			x
Mt. Mercy College		x	
Muhlenberg College	x		
Our Lady of Angels College	x		
Point Park College	x		
Rosemont College	x		
St. Fidelis College and Seminary		x	
St. Francis College		x	
St. Joseph's College		x	
St. Vincent College		x	
Seton Hill College		x	
Susquehanna University			x
Swarthmore College	x		
Thiel College			x
Ursinus College	x		
Villa Maria College		x	
Washington and Jefferson College	x		
Waynesburg College			x
Westminster College			x
Wilkes College	x		
Wilson College	x		
Rhode Island			
Barrington College	x		
Mt. St. Joseph College		x	
Providence College		x	
Salve Regina College		x	
South Carolina			
Allen University			x
Baptist College—Charleston			x
Benedict College			x
Central Wesleyan College			x
Claflin College			x
Coker College for Women	x		

	Independent	Roman Catholic	Other religious affiliation
College of Charleston	x		
Columbia College			x
Converse College	x		
Erskine College			x
Furman University			x
Limestone College	x		
Morris College			x
Newberry College			x
Presbyterian College			x
Vorhees College			x
Wofford College			x
South Dakota			
Dakota Wesleyan University			x
Huron College			x
Mt. Marty College		x	
Sioux Falls College			x
Yankton College	x		
Tennessee			
Belmont College			x
Bethel College			x
Carson Newman College			x
Christian Brothers College		x	
David Lipscomb College			x
Fisk University	x		
King College			x
Knoxville College			x
Lambuth College			x
Lane College			x
Lee College			x
LeMoyne Owen College			x
Lincoln Memorial University	x		
Maryville College			x
Milligan College, Inc.	x		
Siena College		x	
Southern Missionary College			x
Southwestern at Memphis			x

	Independent	Roman Catholic	Other religious affiliation
Tennessee Temple University			x
Tennessee Wesleyan University			x
Trevecca Nazarene College			x
Tusculum College	x		
Union University			x
University of the South			x
William Jennings Bryan College	x		
Texas			
Austin College			x
Bishop College			x
Dallas Baptist College			x
Dominican College		x	
East Texas Baptist College			x
Houston Baptist College			x
Howard Payne College			x
Huston Tillotson College			x
Incarnate Word College		x	
Jarvis Christian College			x
Letourneau College	x		
Mary Hardin Baylor College			x
McMurry College			x
Paul Quinn College			x
St. Edward's University		x	
Southwestern University	x		
Texas College			x
Texas Lutheran College—Main Campus			x
Texas Wesleyan College			x
University of Corpus Christi	x		
University of Dallas		x	
University of St. Thomas		x	
Wayland Baptist College			x
Wiley College			x
Utah			
Westminster College			x

	Independent	Roman Catholic	Other religious affiliation
Vermont			
Bennington College	x		
College of St. Joseph the Provider		x	
Goddard College	x		
Mark Hopkins College	x		
Marlboro College	x		
Middlebury College	x		
Norwich University	x		
St. Michael's College		x	
Trinity College		x	
Windham College	x		
Virginia			
Bridgewater College			x
Eastern Mennonite College			x
Emory and Henry College			x
Hampden Sidney College			x
Hollins College	x		
Lynchburg College	x		
Mary Baldwin College			x
Randolph-Macon College			x
Randolph-Macon Women's College			x
Roanoke College			x
St. Paul's College			x
Sweet Briar College	x		
Virginia Seminary College			x
Virginia Union University			x
Virginia Wesleyan College			x
Washington and Lee College	x		
Washington			
Ft. Wright College — Holy Names		x	
Northwest College			x
St. Martin's College		x	
Whitman College	x		
Whitworth College	x		

	Independent	Roman Catholic	Other religious affiliation
West Virginia			
Alderson Broaddus College			x
Bethany College	x		
Davis and Elkins College			x
Morris Harvey College	x		
Salem College—Main Campus	x		
West Virginia Wesleyan College			x
Wheeling College		x	
Wisconsin			
Alverno College		x	
Beloit College	x		
Cardinal Stritch College		x	
Carroll College			x
Carthage College			x
Dominican College—Racine		x	
Edgewood College		x	
Holy Family College		x	
Lakeland College			x
Lawrence University—Main Campus	x		
Marian College of Fond DuLac		x	
Milton College	x		
Mt. Mary College—Main Campus		x	
Mt. St. Paul College		x	
Mt. Senario College		x	
Northland College	x		
Ripon College	x		
Viterbo College		x	
Puerto Rico			
College of the Sacred Heart		x	

Appendix E: Degrees and Fellowships Earned and Federal Support Received in Independent Liberal Arts Colleges and Universities

The following tables have been prepared by Dr. Howard Bobren, formerly of the Carnegie Commission on Higher Education, from data supplied by sources identified in the tables.

TABLE 1
Earned degrees conferred by independent liberal arts colleges and universities, 1965–1966, and number eligible for initial teacher certification

Size of institution	Bachelor's		1st professional	
	Number of degrees	*Number of institutions conferring*	*Number of degrees*	*Number of institutions conferring*
Under 1,000 total	5,496	60		
1,000–5,000 total	17,871	66	380	9
5,000–10,000 total	7,931	12	461	4
Over 10,000 total	4,072	3	37	1
TOTAL	35,370	141	878	14
Total United States	524,117		31,496	
Percent of total United States	7		3	

SOURCE: *Earned Degrees Conferred 1965–1966,* Office of Education and Teacher Productivity, American Association of Colleges for Teacher Education, 1966.

TABLE 2
Baccalaureate recipients of independent liberal arts colleges receiving doctorates, 1960–1966

Size of institution	Number of doctorates awarded	Number of institutions whose graduates received doctorates
Under 1,000 total	846	49
1,000–5,000 total	4,780	62
5,000–10,000 total	524	12
Over 10,000 total	189	3
TOTAL	6,339	126
Total United States	80,978	
Percent of total United States	8	

SOURCE: National Academy of Science.

Master's		Doctor's		Eligible for initial certification	
Number of degrees	*Number of institutions conferring*	*Number of degrees*	*Number of institutions conferring*	*Number of degrees*	*Number of institutions conferring*
389	11	79	2	550	21
2,857	39	15	4	3,001	36
2,072	10	110	2	2,571	11
1,043	3	—	—	869	2
6,361	63	204	8	6,991	70
140,772		18,239		181,048	
5		1		4	

TABLE 3 **Woodrow Wilson Fellowships awarded, 1945–1967, to graduates of independent liberal arts colleges**	*Number of W. W. Fellowships awarded*	*Number of institutions with recipients*
Size of institution		
Under 1,000 total	346	31
1,000–5,000 total	1,918	55
5,000–10,000 total	93	6
Over 10,000 total	18	3
TOTAL	2,375	95
Total United States	14,326	
Percent of total United States	17	

SOURCE: *Woodrow Wilson Fellows 1945–1967*, Woodrow Wilson Fellowship Foundation.

TABLE 4
*Federal support
to independent
colleges and
universities in
1963 and 1966
(dollars in
thousands)*

	Total		
Independent colleges and universities	*1963*	*1966*	*Percentage of increase*
Under 1,000 total enrollment	4,293	13,822	+222
Number of schools supported	(27)	(63)	+133
1,000–5,000 total enrollment	11,686	27,313	+134
Number of schools supported	(55)	(65)	+18
5,000–10,000 total enrollment	12,342	25,200	+104
Number of schools supported	(9)	(11)	+22
Over 10,000 total enrollment	314	4,400	*
Number of schools supported	(3)	(3)	0
TOTAL	28,635†	70,735‡	+147
Number of schools supported	(94)	(142)	+51
Total United States	1,396,705	3,017,509	+116
Percent of total United States	2†	2‡	

* Greater than 999 percent.

† For 1963, federal support to Catholic higher educational institutions was $35,745,-000 or 2.6% of the total.

‡ For 1966, federal support to Catholic higher educational institutions was $123,-607,000 or 4.1% of the total.

SOURCE: *Federal Support to Universities and Colleges, 1963–66,* National Science Foundation.

Academic science			Nonscience			Percentage of federal funds used for science	
1963	*1966*	*Percentage of increase*	*1963*	*1966*	*Percentage of increase*	*1963*	*1966*
2,163	5,228	+142	2,130	8,594	+303	50	38
(27)	(39)	+44	(6)	(63)	+950*		
10,847	15,467	+43	839	11,846	*	93	57
(52)	(63)	+21	(21)	(65)	+210		
11,764	20,236	+72	578	4,964	+759	95	80
(9)	(11)	+22	(5)	(11)	+120		
208	995	+378	106	3,405	*	66	23
(3)	(3)	0	(2)	(3)	+50		
24,982	41,926	+68	3,653	28,809	+689	87	59
(91)	(116)	+27	(34)	(142)	+318		
1,312,201	2,171,050	+65	84,504	846,459	+902	94	72
2	2		4	3			

TABLE 5
Independent
liberal arts
colleges: 1967
opening fall
enrollment of
resident
undergraduate
and postbacca-
laureate
students

Size of institution	Total enrollment	Undergraduate		
		Full-time		
		Men	Women	Total
Under 1,000 total	42,823	19,939	19,786	39,725
Percent	100	47	46	93
1,000–5,000 total	133,630	56,003	49,553	105,556
Percent	100	42	37	79
5,000–10,000 total	101,629	35,497	19,352	54,849
Percent	100	35	19	54
Over 10,000 total	49,582	15,884	8,699	24,583
Percent	100	32	18	50
TOTAL	327,664	127,323	97,390	224,713
Percent	100	39	30	69
Total U.S.	6,670,416	2,584,952	1,791,603	4,376,555
Percent	100	39	27	66
Percent of total U.S.	5	5	5	5

NOTE: Not all percents add to total percents because of rounding.

SOURCE: *Opening Fall Enrollment in Higher Education, 1967—Supplement A, Undergraduate and Postbaccalaureate Students,* U.S. Government Printing Office, Washington, D.C., 1968.

			Postbaccalaureate					
	Part-time			*Full-time*			*Part-time*	
Men	*Women*	*Total*	*Men*	*Women*	*Total*	*Men*	*Women*	*Total*
940	746	1,686	480	253	733	420	259	679
2	2	4	1	1	2	1	1	2
10,730	7,625	18,355	2,814	941	3,755	3,192	2,772	5,964
8	6	14	2	1	3	2	2	4
17,691	9,549	27,240	4,970	1,373	6,343	8,528	4,399	12,927
18	9	27	5	1	6	9	4	13
9,788	4,300	14,088	1,241	354	1,595	5,838	3,478	9,316
20	9	28	3	1	3	12	7	19
39,149	22,220	61,369	9,505	2,921	12,426	17,978	10,908	28,886
12	7	19	3	1	4	5	3	8
91,384	602,512	1,393,896	356,036	94,400	450,436	277,071	172,458	449,529
12	9	21	5	1	7	4	3	7
5	4	4	3	3	3	6	6	6

Appendix F:
Ninety-nine Colleges in the Document Study for this Book

Ninety-nine colleges responded to our request for documents for use in this study.

The documentary evidence was used in writing vignettes of 20 colleges selected from the 99 for closer study. Selected vignettes were then incorporated into the text of the book.

Statistical material on the 99 colleges was also collected and used for analysis and perspective.

A third type of data came from campus visits made by Morris Keeton and his colleagues. Information from these visits is used in the text in the same way as the vignette material.

The cooperating colleges were:

Adelphi University
Garden City, New York

Amherst College
Amherst, Massachusetts

Antioch College
Yellow Springs, Ohio

Azusa Pacific College
Azusa, California

Barnard College
New York, New York

Bates College
Lewiston, Maine

Bennington College
Bennington, Vermont

Berry College
Mt. Berry, Georgia

Bowdoin College
Brunswick, Maine

Brenau College
Gainesville, Georgia

Bucknell University
Lewisburg, Pennsylvania

Carleton College
Northfield, Minnesota

Chatham College
Pittsburgh, Pennsylvania

Claremont Men's College
Claremont, California

Coker College
Hartsville, South Carolina

Colgate University
Hamilton, New York

College of Charleston
Charleston, South Carolina

College of the Southwest
Hobbs, New Mexico

Colorado College
Colorado Springs, Colorado

Connecticut College
New London, Connecticut

Converse College
Spartanburg, South Carolina

Dartmouth College
Hanover, New Hampshire

Elmira College
Elmira, New York

Fairleigh Dickinson University
Rutherford, New Jersey

Finch College
New York, New York

Fisk University
Nashville, Tennesse

Franklin College
Columbus, Ohio

Gallaudet College
Washington, D.C.

Goddard College
Plainfield, Vermont

Goucher College
Baltimore, Maryland

Grinnell College
Grinnell, Iowa

Hofstra University
Hempstead, New York

Hollins College
Hollins College, Virginia

Husson College
Bangor, Maine

Inter American University of
    Puerto Rico
San German, P.R.

Ithaca College
Ithaca, New York

John Brown University
Siloam Springs, Arkansas

Knox College
Galesburg, Illinois

Lake Erie College
Painesville, Ohio

Lea College
Albert Lea, Minnesota

LeTourneau College
Longview, Texas

Little Rock University
Little Rock, Arkansas

Long Island University
Southamptom, New York

Mackinac College
Mackinac Island, Michigan

Marietta College
Marietta, Ohio

Marlboro College
Marlboro, Vermont

Mills College
Oakland, California

Milton College
Milton, Wisconsin

Monmouth College
Monmouth, Illinois

Morris Harvey College
Charleston, West Virginia

Mount Holyoke College
South Hadley, Massachusetts

Nasson College
Springvale, Maine

New College
Sarasota, Florida

New England College
Henniker, New Hampshire

Norwich University
Northfield, Vermont

Oberlin College
Oberlin, Ohio

Pace College
New York, New York

Pomona College
Claremont, California

Reed College
Portland, Oregon

Rider College
Trenton, New Jersey

Rio Grande College
Rio Grande, Ohio

Ripon College
Ripon, Wisconsin

Rockford College
Rockford, Illinois

Rollins College, Patrick Branch
Patrick Air Force Base, Florida

Rollins College
Winter Park, Florida

Roosevelt University
Chicago, Illinois

Russell Sage College
Troy, New York

St. John's College
Annapolis, Maryland

St. John's College
Santa Fe, New Mexico

St. Lawrence University
Canton, New York

Sarah Lawrence College
Bronxville, New York

Scripps College
Claremont, California

Simmons College
Boston, Massachusetts

Skidmore College
Saratoga Springs, New York

Springfield College
Springfield, Massachusetts

Stephens College
Columbia, Missouri

Swarthmore College
Swarthmore, Pennsylvania

Sweet Briar College
Sweet Briar, Virginia

Transylvania College
Lexington, Kentucky

Trinity College
Hartford, Connecticut

Union College and University
Schenectady, New York

University of Baltimore
Baltimore, Maryland

University of Bridgeport
Bridgeport, Connecticut

University of Tampa
Tampa, Florida

Upper Iowa University
Fayette, Iowa

Utica College (Syracuse University
System)
Utica, New York

Wabash College
Crawfordsville, Indiana

Washington College
Chestertown, Maryland

Washington and Jefferson College
Washington, Pennsylvania

Wellesley College
Wellesley, Massachusetts

Wells College
Aurora, New York

Wesleyan University
Middletown, Connecticut

Western College for Women
Oxford, Ohio

Western New England College
Springfield, Massachusetts

Westmont College
Santa Barbara, California

Wheaton College
Wheaton, Illinois

Wheaton College
Norton, Massachusetts

Whitman College
Walla Walla, Washington

Wilkes College
Wilkes-Barre, Pennsylvania

Acknowledgments

I am indebted to many people for assistance in the preparation of this book. The colleges studied have been generous with their time and information, especially on our visits. Many colleagues have assisted. Data and working papers were provided from the Campus Governance Program of the American Association for Higher Education by Stephen Plumer, Harold Hodgkinson, Ruth Churchill, George C. Stern, Michael Metty, Morton Rauh, Arnold Weber, and Suzanne Imes. Harold Hodgkinson also made available his study *Institutions in Transition;* and George G. Stern, his work for the book *People in Context.* Parker Lichtenstein and Robert MacDowell visited the Associated Colleges of Claremont as part of the study. Judson Jerome shared his studies and experience in visiting other colleges. The Research Department of the American Council on Education and the U.S. Office of Education provided data from their nationwide studies of colleges. Andrew Greeley of the National Opinion Research Center made available data from his studies of alumni. Ronald Wolk provided interview materials from college presidents about the financing of colleges, and Howard Bobren, formerly of the Carnegie Commission on Higher Education, organized certain statistical data. Nancy Teepen served as research associate early in the work, and I later had substantial research assistance from Antioch students Nancy Timmins and Irene Saal and additional help from Nicholas Holt, Judy Supnick, Lock Holmes, Michael McCrory, William Getz, and Lynn Barker. Typing of the manuscript was done by Madaline Robison, Gerda Oldham, Norma Graham, and Gwyn Janes. The project was made possible by support of the Carnegie Commission on Higher Education. My indebtedness to Antioch College shows throughout.

Index

Hilberry, Conrad, 68
Hodgkinson, Harold, 55–57
Humboldt University, 12
Hutchins University, 50

Jerome, Judson, 51
John Brown University, 15–16
Johns Hopkins University, 26

Kalamazoo College, 26, 66
Keeton, Morris, 68, 91–94
Kerr, Clark, 23
Kettering Foundation, 39
Knapp, R. H., 26–28
Knox College, 45, 75, 76

Liaison Committee on Texas Private
    Colleges and Universities, 5
Lichtenstein, Parker, 45–46
Little Rock University, 48

MacDowell, Robert, 46
Mackenzie, Donald M., 83
Marietta College, 26
Mennonites, 20
Miami University of Ohio, 21
Michigan, University of, 50–51
Mill, John Stuart, 18
Mills College, 43–44, 75
Monteith College, 50

National Opinion Research Center (NORC)
    survey of alumni, 32–38, 76
National Science Foundation, 14
New York, financial aid to colleges in, 6
NORC (National Opinion Research Center)
    survey of alumni, 32–38, 76
Norwich University, 47–48

Oberlin College, 8, 26
Ohio State University, 12

Pattillo, Manning, Jr., 83
Pluralism and Partnership (study), 4–5
Princeton University, 3, 8–9, 73, 75
Protestant institutions, 14–16, 21, 28–38

Quakers, 16

Rauh, Morton, 66, 84, 85
Reed College, 26
Reserve Officers Training Corps, 47
Rochester, University of, 26

Saal, Irene, 28*n.*
St. Francis Seminary, 21
Sarah Lawrence College, 46–47, 66–67
Schmidt, George P., 9, 10
Scholastic Aptitude Test (SAT), 15–16,
    45–47
Schultz, Theodore W., 61
Scripps College, 45–46
Southwest Ohio Project for the Study of
    Religion in Higher Education, 20
Stern, George G., 11, 38–41, 85
Swarthmore College, 26

Teepen, Nancy, 28*n.*
Temple University, 20
Texas, support of private colleges in, 4–6
Texas College and University System,
    Coordinating Board of, 4
Tussman program, 51

United Theological Seminary, 21

Vanderbilt University, 3, 73

Wabash College, 26
Wayne State University, 50
Weber, Arnold, 80–81
Wesleyan University, 26, 76
Wheaton College, 14–15

*This book was set in Vladimir by University Graphics,
Inc. It was printed on permanent paper and bound by The
Maple Press Company. The designer was Elliot Epstein.
The editors were Herbert Waentig and Cheryl Allen for
McGraw-Hill Book Company and Verne A. Stadtman and
Margaret Cheney for the Carnegie Commission on Higher
Education. Frank Matonti and Alice Cohen supervised
the production.*

DATE DUE

APR 1 8 2008			
GAYLORD			PRINTED IN U.S.A.